PENGUIN PASSNOTES

Look Back in Anger

Dr Graham Handley has taught and lectured for thirty-
five years. He was Principal Lecturer in English and
Head of Department at the College of All Saints,
Tottenham, and Research Officer in English at Birkbeck
College, University of London. He is a part-time lecturer
in literature with the University of London Department
of Extramural Studies, and has examined at all levels
from CSE to University Honours Degree. He has
published on Mrs Gaskell, George Eliot and Dickens
among others, and has edited *The Mill on the Floss* and
Wuthering Heights for Macmillan, *Daniel Deronda* for the
Clarendon Press and the same novel and Trollope's *The
Three Clerks* for the World's Classics series. He is the
author of the Penguin Passnotes on *The Death of Grass*,
*Far From the Madding Crowd, The Go-Between, The
Pardoner's Tale* and *To Kill a Mockingbird*. He has
written Master Guides on *Middlemarch* and *Silas
Marner*, and Masterstudies of *Barchester Towers* and
Vanity Fair. He is at work on *Tess of the D'Urbervilles*
for the Penguin Critical Studies series.

PENGUIN PASSNOTES

JOHN OSBORNE

Look Back in Anger

GRAHAM HANDLEY

ADVISORY EDITOR: S. H. COOTE M.A., PH.D.

PENGUIN BOOKS

Penguin Books Ltd, 27 Wrights Lane, London W8 5TZ
Viking Penguin Inc., 40 West 23rd Street, New York, New York, 10010, USA
Penguin Books Australia Ltd, Ringwood, Victoria, Australia
Penguin Books Canada Ltd, 2801 John Street, Markham, Ontario, Canada L3R 1B4
Penguin Books (NZ) Ltd, 182–190 Wairau Road, Auckland 10, New Zealand

First published 1990
Copyright © Graham Handley, 1990
All rights reserved

Made and printed in Great Britain by
Richard Clay Ltd, Bungay, Suffolk

Filmset in 10/12 pt Monophoto Ehrhardt

Contents

For Janet and Sancha, with love

To the Student

This book is designed to help you with your GCSE English Literature Examination. It contains a synopsis of the plot, a detailed account of it and a commentary on its characters, themes and structure as well as issues raised by the text.

Page references are to the Faber paperback edition of the play.

When you use this book remember that it is no more than an aid to your study. It will help you to find passages quickly, and perhaps it will give you some ideas for coursework essays and the examination paper. But remember: *This book is not a substitute for reading the text, and it is your knowledge of that text and your responses to it that matter.* These are the things that the examiners are looking for, and they are also the things that will give you the most pleasure. Show your knowledge and appreciation to the examiner, and show them clearly.

Introduction
John Osborne: Biographical Notes

John Osborne was born in Fulham, London, in 1929, the son of a Welsh commercial artist and a barmaid who was celebrated for her dexterity in juggling glasses and pouring from four at the same time. John's father was chronically ill for a number of years, eventually dying in 1940: the marriage was unhappy, with mother and son moving from lodging to lodging, often staying only a short while in each one. This meant that John Osborne's education was piecemeal, and he himself suffered from a number of illnesses, including a severe bout of glandular fever.

He has left a full, humorous, abrasively honest account of the first twenty-seven years of his life in his autobiography, *A Better Class of Person* (1981). This goes up to the writing of *Look Back in Anger* and its acceptance (after other rejections) for production at the Royal Court Theatre. You are strongly recommended to read this autobiography, or at least to dip into it. Much of it has direct connections with *Look Back in Anger* (remember that Osborne dedicated the play to his father). But there is an even stronger reason than that for reading it. It is a wonderful social, moral, period account in its own right – independent, provocative, irreverent and *truthful*. Osborne has no time for fakes, fools, hypocrites, and he says so. His account of his childhood is often frightening, often sad, sometimes funny: it is never dull, always vivid, vital and immediate.

The sense of period which characterizes the play is potently present in the autobiography. There is the claustrophobia of home or school, family pressures, and the vivid recall of being bullied (by both sexes, different schools): there is the clichéd patriotism and trite inadequacy of a poor public school. The immediacy which Osborne captures in his brilliantly selective look back runs through the whole book. His own interests in music-hall, in radio programmes and in films of the period are nostalgically, movingly, recaptured. He looks back to the different family characters and their family legends which informed his childhood. His early experiences in publishing and the theatre are brilliantly observed: his relationships, whether with his mother or his friends, are unsparingly revealed. He tells how he borrowed his persecuting cousin Tony's surname (Porter) 'for a character in a play'. Certainly parts of his life fed into *Look Back in Anger*. But it would be wrong to identify Osborne overmuch with Jimmy Porter. Jimmy is a character in a play made by Osborne: when I first saw it, over thirty years ago, I felt that he spoke with the authentic voice of his time. I still feel that. *Look Back in Anger* has outlasted that time because the dramatic experience it conveys – a compound of anger, conflict, sadness, loss, uncertainty, humour – is relevant for our time and, I believe, for all time. It is uncompromising, direct, a searingly honest play.

Other Reading: two or three plays by Osborne, notably *The Entertainer* (1957), with that great survivor of music-hall days, Archie Rice, and *Luther* (1961), based on the life of Martin Luther. He has also adapted Ibsen's *Hedda Gabler* and Oscar Wilde's *The Picture of Dorian Gray* and has written for television and films as well as the theatre.

Synopsis

Jimmy Porter and his wife Alison are living in a Midland town. They have a flat which they share with Jimmy's friend Cliff who, unlike Jimmy, has not had a university education. Alison is from a superior social class, something which Jimmy resents. He often attacks her verbally, and Cliff acts as peacemaker. He is obviously fond of Alison in a friendly and sympathetic way. Jimmy also attacks Cliff from time to time, finding his wife and his friend apathetic. He is insecure, unsure of his position in society, resenting the middle-class way of life as epitomized by Alison's family. We sense too a fear and resentment of women which he releases in these attacks on Alison.

The men tease one another and, during a bout of horseplay between them, Jimmy pushes Cliff against the ironing board which Alison is using. She burns her arm. Jimmy is concerned, Alison hurt and angry and, when Jimmy leaves the room, Cliff consoles her. Alison confides to Cliff that she is going to have a baby, but that she hasn't been able to bring herself to tell Jimmy. She is frightened of his reaction, that he may feel trapped by the news. When Jimmy returns there is more horseplay. Cliff goes out to get cigarettes, and Jimmy tells Alison that he is sorry. They play their own private game of pretending that they are bears and squirrels. With the return of Cliff, who announces a phone call from 'Helena Something' Jimmy's mood worsens. Alison takes the call and tells them that her friend Helena Charles is coming to stay. This provokes a wicked outburst from Jimmy, an attack on Alison in which he hopes that if she has a child it will die.

After Helena has been there for two weeks Alison tells her how she came to meet Jimmy, how her parents opposed their wish to marry, how they married despite this, and what happened afterwards. Alison also confides in Helena about the fantasy world of bears and squirrels. Jimmy's attacks now take in Helena. He also gives a moving account of how, as a small boy, he watched his father die. When he learns that

Alison and Helena are going to church he feels betrayed. Another telephone call interrupts the action. This time it is for Jimmy. After he leaves Helena reveals that she has sent a telegram to Alison's father asking him to come and take Alison home. She does not object to going. But when Jimmy returns he is angered by the fact that Alison will not come to see his friend Hugh's dying mother.

When Alison's father arrives he proves to be rather different from what we expected. He too looks back to the past. Alison now has a moment of decision about leaving. When she goes, Helena stays behind. She has obviously contrived the situation so that she will be alone with Jimmy. Cliff indicates that he understands why Helena has acted in this way, and he certainly disapproves of it. He is bitter, for we know that he is fond of Alison. The latter has written to Jimmy explaining why she has left. Cliff has the letter, but he passes it to Helena to give to Jimmy when he returns after his visit to Hugh's mum.

Jimmy is angry and disgusted when he reads the letter. Helena now tells him that Alison is going to have a baby. He is now both despairing and hurt. He tells Helena to get out. She slaps his face, but then kisses him passionately and draws him to her.

Several months later we find Jimmy, Cliff and Helena in the flat. Now it is Helena who is doing the ironing. She seems able to cope rather better than Alison did. Jimmy and Cliff go into a comic song-and-dance act modelled on two comedians of the period. Helena is the audience. The two men indulge in horseplay, but Helena, unlike Alison earlier, is not injured. Cliff says that he has decided to leave. Although Jimmy mocks and gets at him for his decision, it is obvious that there is a real bond of friendship between the two men. When Cliff exits there is a passionate scene between Helena and Jimmy. But just as they are about to go out for a drink, Alison, looking 'rather ill', comes in. Jimmy goes out and leaves the two women together.

Their conversation and what results from it brings the play to its conclusion. Although Helena has given in to her sexual need for Jimmy, she feels that she is acting wrongly. This means that Alison's return has provided her with the excuse that she needs to leave Jimmy. Alison has lost her baby, but feels compelled to come back to Jimmy despite her misgivings. Helena takes the decision to leave, and decides to summon Jimmy in to tell him. He intuitively knows of the death of the child, and accepts what Helena has to say. When Helena goes Alison and Jimmy are left together. Alison tells him that she has suffered all that he wished upon her, and that now she is grovelling as he wanted. They have the fantasy of the bears and squirrels left to them, and escape into it.

An Account of the Plot

ACT I

The stage directions are explicit and detailed, and should be read carefully wherever they occur. There is an immediate impression of claustrophobia, of too much having to be packed into the one room which constitutes the Porters' flat. A note of pathos is sounded, a feeling that we are about to enter into frustrated lives, indicated perhaps by the description of the furniture, which ranges from the 'old' to the 'shabby'. Notice how accurately, choosing his words with careful weight and precision, Osborne describes and defines his central character, Jimmy Porter. Jimmy's friend Cliff is given less space but there is a similar focus and concrete emphasis: what Osborne calls his 'natural counterpoint' to Jimmy is to be developed and demonstrated throughout the arguments and interactions which follow.

Despite the fact that her personality is 'elusive', we get a definite sense of Alison's presence. Osborne uses connected musical associations – polyphony, key, orchestration – to emphasize the fact that her personality is 'drowned' by the men. And the class differences, which are a running theme in the play, are hinted at in Alison's appearance. The fact that she is wearing Jimmy's shirt is also important. We should also note the unusual words (polyphony, equivocation) to get just the right emphasis (look up these words in the dictionary). This is the mark of Osborne's craftsmanship before the play proper begins: for the reader/watcher, it is a considered building of atmosphere. The silence broken only by the thud of the iron is dramatically effective (notice how Osborne makes use of noise throughout the play). We are keyed up for speech to begin.

Once Jimmy speaks we sense the boredom and frustration. He has a ready sarcasm, seen here in his remark about the use of French in English criticism. Cliff plays up to being called ignorant by replying in Cockney dialect. Alison is baited by Jimmy's reference to the 'White Woman's Burden'. It is the first literary association, a twisting of the title of Kipling's poem 'The White Man's Burden', and it is also the first of Jimmy's anti-colonial statements. He is exasperated at getting no verbal response from Alison, and now indulges in a routine of mockery. Here we note that Cliff, the other member of the unwilling audience, tries to protect Alison from further attack. There is a mixture of tension and buffoon-like comedy. Cliff, in fact, matches Jimmy in some of the exchanges. His fantasy about Jimmy and the *News of the World* gives Osborne the opportunity to parody that newspaper, which was regarded at the time as being outrageously outspoken.

The bickering over tea shows Jimmy's restlessness and his need for attention. Yet we get the impression that the three of them fit together. Jimmy's aggression and provocation are balanced by Cliff's sentimental attitude towards Alison. At the same time we are aware of the strong, compulsive sexual attraction between Alison and Jimmy when their eyes meet.

The reactionary remarks reported of the Bishop of Bromley leave first Alison and then Cliff apathetic. There could be no greater spur for Jimmy, who can now attack Alison's father and the supposedly entrenched right-wing views that he holds. He is always intent upon provoking a reaction, particularly in Alison. His anecdote about the woman who is injured declaring herself for God at the Evangelist meeting – probably a reference to the popular American preacher Billy Graham – is a sick joke meant to stir things up.

It is obvious that Jimmy is greatly at variance with his time, but his constant need to provoke, harass, bully, show a deep-seated uncertainty about life, relationships, himself: there is a recurring need of reassurance. The suggestion that they should go to the pictures (p. 15) only moves him to another outburst. Then the trapped rebel goes on to attack J. B. Priestley, the author whose fireside-chat type radio broadcasts boosted morale in wartime Britain. Jimmy finds his cosy image offensive.

The sequence in which Cliff takes his trousers off (p. 16) would be acceptable in the farces of the time: it is somewhat daring in a 'serious' play. Osborne uses it naturally and uninhibitedly. But the tensions here don't arise from this situation. They derive from what Osborne calls Jimmy's pursuit of Alison, his deliberate, excessive attempts to provoke her to anger. Then he snatches at the idea of listening to a concert, but this is only a jumping-off point for a sustained and embittered attack on the preservation of middle-class values as symbolized by Daddy and his past way of life. The indictment of the American Age, the pop culture of films and music for example (p. 17), is perhaps as relevant today as it was in the mid-1950s.

After the mention of Webster Alison begins to get her own back with her insinuations about Madeline. Jimmy backs away from confrontation here by returning to the concert and invoking the next day's work. He soon leaves this and switches to a mood of more calculated wounding by praising Madeline's animation. Alison's 'tired' appeal reflects her inward suffering, but Jimmy's response is merely to extend his attack on her family. He concentrates on brother Nigel: 'Vaguery in the Field' (for the obvious 'Bravery') reflects the blending of satirical and personal humour and anger which Jimmy achieves. But when he has finished he cannot estimate the effect of his 'rhetoric' because there is silence, which is sufficiently deflating in itself. He soon gets his second wind. Alison's parents are again on the receiving end, for Jimmy asserts that there is nothing to which they wouldn't stoop despite their veneer of civilized behaviour (p. 21).

Jimmy is now beginning to pick up in inspiration, and he plays on the word 'pusillanimous' with some wit and verve, reasonably obvious but genuinely funny. He attacks certain types of Hollywood film (the sketch he has now plunged into is a parody of a film anyway), watching all the time for Alison to break. She survives the crisis by her practical application to ironing Cliff's trousers. Such is Jimmy's state that it is noticeable how easily distracted he is – whether by Cliff crumpling the newspaper, or Alison's electric iron supposedly interfering with the quality of the reception on the wireless set.

The next launch starts with a particularized attack on Alison's habits and then proceeds with great bitterness and anger to a more generalized attack on the habits of women (p. 24). When Jimmy goes on to recount his experiences of the girls in the flat above him he employs the imagery of war ('a sort of assault course' and 'like a medieval siege') to describe what is for him the battle of the sexes. We get the impression that he is very scared of women. The sound of the bells causes him to switch the area of his attack yet again. With his anti-establishment views, he naturally assaults the church, here as well as later. Cliff tries to turn his anger, and this meets with a music-hall, cross-talk-comedian kind of response from Jimmy, who is resilient and adaptable when it suits him to be. The joke between them evokes the atmosphere of the 1950s, the small dance-hall fantasy having sexual associations, for example in the phrase 'only in the mating season' (p. 25), the standard joke-cliché of the time.

The fooling, the mock-fight, misfires badly (p. 26). Alison is hurt, and this when she is trying not to break down anyway. Jimmy leaves at a nod from Cliff, who comforts Alison instead of Jimmy, a reversal of the situation we might expect between husband and wife. Is the tenderness that Cliff shows to Alison something that Jimmy is unable to give her? The frustration and despair that she feels is fully conveyed as, left alone on stage for a moment, she can only say 'Oh God!' (p. 27). But Cliff's attentions to her as he tries to ease the pain, his natural warmth, sympathy and affection for her, all these move her. When he massages her neck it is an extension of his tenderness, an attempt to induce a more relaxed physical and emotional state in her. It works, despite her concern to know where Jimmy is and what he is doing: it is as if she can't – and at this stage she can't – escape from him.

But the interplay of sympathy between herself and Cliff makes him confiding and her responsive: each is confessing needs, dependence and frustration to the other. At this moment of sympathetic interaction Osborne is giving us another insight into the way people are. Cliff's statement (p. 27), as we have seen, is an honest appraisal of himself: Alison's response is to look back in anger, frustration, anguish at her life with Jimmy.

There is a terrible despair in her tone (p. 28). Cliff's words reflect his own feeling for her as well as his repugnance at the situation between them (Alison and Jimmy), but he cannot stop the flow – the burn seems to have unleashed Alison's pent-up feelings. Cliff's practical idea of bandaging her arm is an attempt to put the physical need before the emotional one – a vain attempt, as it proves. Alison reveals so much about the nature of a close relationship, for example, the reflex natural antipathies which exist between herself and Jimmy, her remaining silent, pretending not to listen by way of provocation, instead of understanding and agreeing with what Jimmy was saying – though in fact she did agree. Osborne is probing the nature of intimate, claustrophobic human relationships with deadly – and deadly accurate – insight.

In Alison's case, so potent is the present that she cannot remember a particular point in the past when she felt young: this is the terrible price of responsibility, adulthood, economic, social and sexual pressures. She shows her own dependence in her questions and the voicing of her own fear.

The actions of bandaging are subordinate to Alison's need to tell Cliff (not Jimmy) of her pregnancy: she obviously fears how Jimmy might have reacted had she told him. That fear is filled with unvoiced questions, some soon to be articulated, others not. And perhaps we are aware, if we lived through the cliché-situation films of the period, that Osborne is here deliberately reversing a current scene, one where the conventional little wife tells her husband that she is going to have a baby. This usually evoked a tender and protective response which was ridiculous in its sentimentality, or an unbelieving or surprised response of an equally false nature. Here the quality of the realism is evident.

There is too an ominous association, unconscious on Cliff's part, but highly charged as regards the audience, when he mentions 'scissors' after a few moments. It is almost as if the baby, like a part of the bandage, can be cut away. Cliff, though he has expressed doubt about whether he can carry on watching Alison and Jimmy in conflict, now takes on the role of the friend who *knows* that Jimmy loves Alison, and therefore all will be well if she tells him. Alison's reading of the situation is tellingly accurate, her forecast based on her knowledge of Jimmy's moods and his own particular feelings, the complexity of his emotional responses. Again we are aware that Osborne is exploring and exposing the nature of intimacy.

Alison looks back, not so much in anger as concerned to define what Jimmy was and is. Part of Jimmy's resentment of her was because she was a virgin (p. 30). It is typical of his inverted attitude towards life. Yet even as Alison is telling Cliff this, she is aware that both of them know that Jimmy would appreciate what she is saying: it makes him a positive and *angry* character whose morality is strongly individual and involves the rejection of conventional standards. We also get the feeling that Cliff gets some pleasure from being thought 'common'. His reiteration that Alison should tell Jimmy about the baby is an underlining of his faith in their love.

At this point Jimmy enters, and again we notice that Osborne is using, with a difference, a commonplace of the cinema, the entrance of the husband who catches his best friend with his wife. The author, before the end of the first act, has so convinced us of the essential truth of the relationships he is depicting, that we accept the actions and reactions of his characters without question.

Very interesting, and dramatically effective, is the stage direction which shows their awareness of Jimmy. After a moment Cliff glances naturally at him, Alison's head still resting against his cheek. It is as if they are presenting a mirror-image of a tranquil and undemanding relationship in contrast to the reality of the one between Alison and Jimmy. The latter is right in character, not looking at Alison when he inquires about her burn: he even plays up to what he knows is expected of him by suggesting that Alison and Cliff go to bed together.

Soon Cliff and Jimmy are moving back into their relationship. Cliff kids Jimmy in his 'Puritan' remark (p. 31); this cunningly looks back to Jimmy's 'private morality' which Alison has defined. Though a light tone has been established, Jimmy throws in another bitter aside about Mummy and Daddy. It is not just bitter. Jimmy feels that he is much more enlightened and broadly tolerant than they are, and suggests that if they were to see Cliff and Alison embracing they would be shocked. The idea of this – and he creates a vivid visual picture – releases the tensions of his mood and he becomes more relaxed. He turns his verbal spotlight on Cliff and the latter, true to the give-and-take nature of their friendship, responds in an appropriately mouse-like manner.

Cliff even rises to a feeble pun – 'mourris' for 'mouse' – thus drawing down upon himself Jimmy's contempt. The humour now takes a physical turn again. Cliff grabs Jimmy's foot and attempts to initiate a grotesque version of the traditional (Morris) dance. He also twice refers to Jimmy as a bear: it is obvious that he is using the private escape language of the Jimmy–Alison fantasy. The reaction of Alison is shown in the stage direction. It reveals her insecurity and fear. This horseplay marks the restoration of normality for her – but what a normality! Osborne is here, as ever, conveying the deep pathos of the situation.

In the preceding verbal and physical interaction, we had almost forgotten the crisis, so brilliantly does Osborne create a compelling, absorbing atmosphere on stage. That atmosphere now changes suddenly as we see the other side of Jimmy. The change of mood is still coloured by frustration and anger, from the pathos and humility of his apology to his self-admissions of violence, sexual drive, claustrophobia.

The strong sexual attraction that Jimmy feels is not diminished, only increased, by these frustrations: Jimmy acknowledges the effects of the commonplace, the 'trivialities' (p. 33), habits and rituals on people's lives. The mention of 'old stock' is poignant and weighted, for Jimmy is using a term associated with the sweet-barrow and himself at the same time. Ironically, Alison herself comes from the 'old stock', the superior Mummy and Daddy so despised by Jimmy.

When Jimmy puts his head against Alison's belly he is behaving like a child in need of affection and reassurance; for audience and reader this is moving because he is so *physically* close to the child he doesn't know about. This shows Osborne's craftsmanship at its best, for by holding him in this way Alison is behaving like the mother she half fears to be. It is a powerful dramatic moment, made more passionate and sexual in the next few lines.

Jimmy's question about Cliff's 'don't forget' puts us on the edge of Alison's confession, but the opportunity passes as Jimmy plunges into a self-pitying look back in anger at the 'friends' of the past who are now merely names to him (p. 34). But it is not just self-pity: there is always method and motive in whatever Osborne does. For instance, we learn much of the past and how Jimmy came to acquire the sweet-stall. Above that, Osborne employs the brilliant device of making a character who never appears in the on-stage action of the play – Hugh's mum – a major influence on its events and situations. Again we note another facet of Jimmy's character: he is loyal, concerned, committed, but we can also see from Alison's reaction that she fears his commitment. She is much relieved when he initiates their bear-and-squirrel fantasy. The mimes and movements are sensual, the mood giving Alison the opportunity, as she feels, to tell Jimmy that she is pregnant. The pathos of 'Everything just seems all right suddenly' when a moment ago it was all wrong, deepens with the re-entrance of Cliff and his news that Alison is wanted on the phone by Helena (p. 35). The moment – if there is ever a right moment – has gone. Helena, from Jimmy's point of view, is his natural enemy anyway because of her class background. He is threatened by the coming of this outsider. He cites Shakespeare for good measure – 'the expense of spirit' – for Jimmy has a word-processor's literary memory. It is the mark of his education, a badge worn rather self-consciously, a kind of compensation for the class inferiority which he feels.

Jimmy who, a few minutes earlier, was full of his male sexual lust, now proceeds to invoke homosexual associations by way of underlining his anti-woman obsession. A 'scoutmaster' is often associated in the cheap scandal consciousness with an interest in boys: 'old Gide', the great French writer (1869–1951) was known to be homosexual. Jimmy further develops his theme by referring to the 'Greek Chorus boys'. The chorus in a Greek tragedy commented on the characters in the play and their actions (Jimmy is almost his own chorus in *this* play), but we should remember too that the Greeks regarded love between men as a more elevated form of love than the sexual expression between man and woman. Jimmy is really saying, in this strongly anti-feminine diatribe, that though homosexuals may suffer moral and social condemnation, at least they have 'revolutionary fire' (p. 35) to be different from those who are 'normal' and dull.

With his mind flitting over Greek tragedy he comes almost naturally to the 'tragic hero' and then perhaps subconsciously to Oedipus ('a man with a strawberry mark'), the subject of tragedies by Sophocles (*c*. 496–406 BC). The birthmark provides the proof of his terrible guilt: Oedipus, ignorant in each case of their identity, killed his father and, later, married his own mother. Jimmy has a great capacity for self-dramatics and claims that he, like Oedipus, has been singled out.

Jimmy's restlessness, his inward tension causing his mind to move in a number of directions, is seen in his reflex action of looking through Alison's handbag (p. 36). He is still on the homosexual tack though, as his reference to Michelangelo shows. The celebrated Italian artist, sculptor and poet (1475–1564) was also homosexual, and the use of the term 'Brigade' (military/war imagery again) is an assertion that homosexuals stick together. He is reminding us of the International Brigades which fought in the Spanish Civil War (1936–9) on the government side against the Fascists under General Franco. Jimmy, mocking the jargon, is implying that he would seem an extremist to a homosexual. And with his natural facility for following out ideas, he links this to the Revolution and his own fate should that occur.

When Cliff engages him on the subject of Alison's handbag, we see his insecurity and possessiveness exposed once again. His searches reflect his need for reassurance. But there is an ominous association with the political and moral climate of the period. Betrayal within the family, children betraying parents, the betrayal of Jews to the Nazis, these are the commonplaces of Hitler's abuse of power in Germany immediately before and during the Second World War. In fictional terms one of the major influences on the post-war period of which Osborne is writing is George Orwell's *1984* (1948), where privacy is impossible and betrayal rules. Osborne is conveying in miniature the uncertainties and fears of the period in Jimmy's own quest here for identity and certainty. He is cynical, and expects to find 'trouble', according to Cliff (p. 36). He represents himself as being violent in order to work off his anger at Alison giving way to Helena.

There then follows the terrible, unconscious anticipation of what actually happens, the death of Alison's child. Here Jimmy's ferocity of language in the expressed wish is an attempt to bring Alison to life: ironically, after the loss of the baby, it is to bring them back into life together. Most effective here is the running dramatic irony, since he does not know what audience and reader do know, that Alison is going to have a baby. He now has to express, in a vicious and frightening extension of the animal imagery of the play, his fear of women as personified by Alison. The implication is that when she is aroused she is a python, and that he is devoured whole. The irony is that the 'bulge' *is* him, the child he has fathered. And at this moment he is revealing his own subconscious wish to return to the security and protection of the womb and thus escape the responsibilities, the ties, the burdens of adult life. Osborne has achieved here a superbly condensed effect – man and child are linked biologically yet separated by the physical fact of the child's existence in the womb. The secret of her womb remains as Jimmy rants on while Cliff, in his usual role, is watching Jimmy and Alison destroy each other.

ACT II SCENE i

The sameness of the scene is given a considered stress as the act opens, but the importance of change is registered at once in the person of Helena. The differences between Alison and Helena are marked. For the reader of the play the stage directions are once again the important index to personality: note particularly words like 'matriarchal' and the finely ironic 'the royalty of her middle-class womanhood'. These serve to imprint Helena's personality on us before she begins to speak out. She is used to being treated with some deference, something that is obviously going to sharpen Jimmy's anger and aggression. We get too the suggestion of a 'stage presence' (after all, she is an actress) with the mention of 'cat-calls'. Her long exchange with Alison enables the latter to tell the story of her meeting with Jimmy and of the subsequent opposition they encountered from her parents. This dialogue between the two women forms an effective contrast with all that has gone before, the even flow replacing the ranting and the horseplay which have characterized so much of the action. It has to be admitted that the dramatic temperature has fallen.

The fact that the women shared similar backgrounds once again provides a contrast with their present experience. Alison observes that Helena has 'settled in so easily', an ominous but unconscious anticipation that Helena is later to replace her in the home. Helena is certainly repelled, but she is also fascinated, inquisitive, and helpful as far as Alison is concerned. And all the while we are aware that Jimmy, though off-stage, is far from silent. The trumpet, like the bells earlier, shows that the dissonance of these lives is being emphasized through the sounds.

Alison's tension shows again. Now she fears that the neighbours will complain about the noise that Jimmy is making. But Helena, while expressing horror, is obviously reacting sexually to Jimmy's violent use of the trumpet. She compares it to sex and violation. Meanwhile, her inquisitiveness is seen in her questions about Cliff. She seems to be lacking the broad understanding to accept a relationship between a man and a woman which is not based on sex. She doubts Alison's version of the 'fond' feeling that she and Cliff have for each other. That fondness, which Helena finds 'simple', provides some of the few tranquil moments in the play.

Helena continues, cynical, doubtful, probing, and Alison does her best to define Jimmy's 'allegiances' (p. 42), his beliefs, his loves and his values. But since his loyalties take in so much, Alison confesses that she cannot cope with them: perhaps even more important than this is her statement that she does not believe that Jimmy is 'right'. She goes on to indicate that her relationship with Cliff is based on Cliff's 'kind and lovable' nature *and* on Jimmy's own acceptance of his allegiance to Cliff and of Cliff's allegiance to him.

Once Alison tells Helena of how she went to live with Jimmy in Hugh's flat, we note that the initial situation was similar to the present one before the arrival of Helena – one woman, two men – almost as if Jimmy needs the cushion of the presence of another male. Hugh was certainly no Cliff and, despite Jimmy's wish for a close relationship between Alison and Hugh, they didn't get on. For Alison, the wedding-night memory of the three of them trying to get drunk on cheap port is sordid. Jimmy's allegiance to Hugh has pitchforked Alison into a situation which is beyond her: we register his depression at his failure to make everything right between Alison and Hugh.

The class demarcation lines are clearly drawn, but Alison obviously had too much pride to go back to her familiar world. The emphasis on the General Election and her brother Nigel (p. 43) is a further indication of the distance between her world and Jimmy's. Notice how the alliteration of 'soft', 'squeamish' and 'snobbish' contributes to the effect. Alison, once she gets going, has a control of language which is direct, dependent on cliché ('burnt my boats') and association rather than on the rhetoric and literary analogies which Jimmy employs. Her account reflects the edge of violence which she lived on in her new world ('a jungle'): the use of words like 'savagery' and 'hostage' is a further extension of the 'war' imagery of the play and exemplifies the atmosphere of her life. Now it is Alison who is looking back, in anguish more than in anger.

There is an interesting indication of the self-protectiveness of the middle classes: Alison has signed away her money, with the result that Jimmy and Hugh feel obliged to exact some revenge. Another war image – 'A brilliant campaign' – shows the destructive but organized nature of their action. And that image is followed by others of a like nature which show them carrying the fight to the wealthy, privileged, upper-middle-class families of the West End and other prosperous parts of London.

It is an instance of the class war being given a grotesque twist. The barbarous associations with Hugh ensure that the contrast with the peaceful and kindly Cliff is being emphasized. Alison had found herself completely caught up in their activities and unable to escape. In fact her past and her present are linked by this strong sense of being trapped. Her account to Helena of being 'unsettled' when the family came back from India, her look at her own position then, followed by the overwhelming, fated and inescapable draw towards Jimmy when she met him at a party – all this shows that Alison in her own way is a rebel. She is obstinately committed to what she decided to take on.

The strength of her sexual response to Jimmy should not be underestimated: it is seen in 'Everything about him seemed to burn', together with the ironic use of the knightly comparison. There could hardly be anyone less chivalrous than Jimmy, and his determination to put down her brother Nigel by roughing up his political meetings has an ominous ring. The Hugh–Jimmy split is a classical instance of those who are basically in sympathy being divided on an important issue. Jimmy's real security thereafter is to stay and fight on, almost as if he cannot let go of the conflict by which he lives. By Jimmy's standards of anti-establishment commitment, Hugh opts out, and the reference to 'Dame Alison's Mob' (the upper classes) shows that Hugh feels that post-war England has reverted to pre-war England in terms of its class structure.

Notice that Jimmy is opposed to Hugh leaving his mother. His loyalty to her is part of his character. The reference to the New Millennium (p. 46), the state of perfection which would be achieved with the second coming of Christ, shows that Alison has an aptitude for sarcasm. The reaction of Hugh's mother – she never appears on stage – is very important, for we sense that because she blames the presence of Alison for what has happened, so Alison in her turn may feel that Jimmy will blame her too. If she had not come on the scene, then the division between Jimmy and Hugh, culminating in Hugh's decision to leave, might never have occurred. We already know the high premium that Jimmy places on friendship.

Helena now shows just how bossy she can be: she virtually tells Alison what to do. There is genuine pathos when Alison, knowing that Helena is suggesting that the baby *might* not be Jimmy's, says

'I've never really wanted anyone else'. The reference to the 'mad-house' is accompanied by an off-stage '*trumpet crescendo*', almost as if Jimmy has heard Helena's remark. When Alison confides to her their private fantasy of the squirrels and bears, Helena responds with a characteristically unusual but recognizably middle-class affectation — 'fey' — an inadequate and refined word. Alison's revelation carries with it a heart-rending pathos, for the implication is surely that the fantasy is their only mode of sanity. Her account of their escape into it, with terms varying from 'priesthole' to 'silly symphony', is very moving. It conveys the nature of human suffering as shown in their two lives, with the implication that reality is for so many of us unbearable.

This seems to galvanize Helena into assertiveness. Or is it the fact that subconsciously she wants Jimmy? Osborne is adept at winding the audience up to the climax and then ... Well, here Cliff enters before Alison can respond to Helena's pressure. His entrance provokes another crisis, for with Helena's announcement that she and Alison are going to church — just as Jimmy is about to come in — there is bound to be trouble. The women have reverted to their middle-class practice and convention. Cliff tries to act as peacemaker, sensing the eruption to come. He makes much of having tea, kids Jimmy about his trumpet, but already the squabbling has started (p. 48). Jimmy is warming to his work, and starts on his 'wife's friends' (with obvious allusion to Helena). Alison and Helena, perhaps conscious of the likely impact of what they are about to do, remain initially silent. Jimmy is now well into his stride on the subject of middle-class intellectuals — he is getting at Cliff too for his lack of positive commitment — who discuss sex in a manner removed from warmth and experience (p. 49). He refers to the 'Art of Fugue' as a measure of their attitude. This is a collection of musical pieces by Johann Sebastian Bach (1685–1750) noted for their intricacy, a fugue being a difficult musical form.

Notice the range of Jimmy's language, with 'meringues' and 'tom-toms' used here to put down Alison and her kind. The second has tribal associations of a primitive nature which Jimmy chooses to connect with the middle classes and Alison's parents in particular. Note too his outward over-politeness to Helena. He is soon into his music-hall routine, calling up again his punning on 'pusillanimous'.

The song-title, itself ridiculous, is the poor-witty-hoping-for-a-laugh line of the comedian. It launches Jimmy into the comic-song monologue which requires no response from the others (p. 50). The recitation of the lyrics is a calculated enjoyment for Jimmy, for he gets a kick out of the fact that the women are being forced to suffer them in silence. The lyrics are pacifically praised by Cliff, but they are expressive of sexual boredom and the need to drink oneself into a state in order to escape from the demands of sex. The 'old python coil' reminds us of his earlier feelings of being eaten alive by Alison, while the hetero/metero rhyme is typical of the song-writing of the day with its play on words. Of course, it is a parody of a popular song.

Jimmy addresses himself to Helena, now his chief antagonist. The references to Dante and T. S. Eliot lead to *The Waste Land* (1922), the most influential poem of the twentieth century. Jimmy's clever-clever improvisation converts this into 'The Cess Pool', the title suggesting the disgust with contemporary life which is Jimmy's constant refrain and Eliot's part concern in his poem. 'There are no dry cleaners in Cambodia' is deliberate doggerel. Cliff uses the current slang of the time to cap what Jimmy is saying. To be 'dropped in it' means here to suffer because of what you have done.

When Helena intervenes Jimmy finds that he has got the conflict that he wanted. Helena has indeed risen to the bait and Jimmy rises in his turn. This time he chooses a known class literary reference, to the eccentric and overpowering Lady Bracknell in Oscar Wilde's famous comedy, *The Importance of Being Earnest*. His idea is obviously to connect Alison and Helena with a dated upper-crust society. When Helena says that they are going to church Jimmy is unprepared. He feels betrayed, but although he turns on Alison he knows that the power struggle is now between himself and Helena. As he sees it, Helena is determined to get Alison back into the ways of conformity and convention from which he has 'rescued' her. When Alison breaks out, undertakes her own passionate look back in anger, Jimmy realizes that his power over her has not gone, that their anger, bitterness, conflict, constitute the bond between them.

It leads him to calm assertion rather than ranting denunciation. He attacks Alison's mother in a calculating way to shock Helena, to make *her* respond, feel, hate, reject in return. He uses the most grotesque and exaggerated comparisons. The idea of a rhinoceros in labour is complemented by references to over-indulgence in food and drink. Jimmy goes deliberately over the top in physical and sexual innuendo about the Bombay brothel and the sailor's arms, though the idea that Alison's mother is there spying on them is audacious and impossible. Jimmy is rarely at a loss when it comes to imaginative coinages, and he wittily picks up the catch-phrase of a contemporary comedian, Sandy Powell's 'Can you 'ear me, mother?' It is tellingly appropriate to his rejection of Alison's mother, since Powell was a north country comedian whose accent epitomized northern independence of southern superiority, something which Jimmy would appreciate. By the time he gets to the end of his diatribe he is using terms like 'the old grey mare' (a real knight would have a white charger) to show how hard he fought to get Alison and how the odds of doing so were against him. The reference here is to a popular song of the time.

Cliff continues to be the restraining influence. Jimmy is determined to break Alison by his extreme language against her mother. When he wishes her dead Cliff tries to intervene – he and Helena are watching tensely to see how much Alison can take – but he is easily, savagely pushed away by Jimmy. Jimmy goes for the 'knock-out', vividly imagining the worms on the corpse of Alison's mother made constipated by her toughness and bulk. His familiar facility with language – the punning link of 'purgatives' and 'purgatory' – is seen again here, and he draws from Helena the positive response of contempt. Note that another 'sporting' image is used by Osborne to underline Jimmy's attitude – '*He can feel her struggling on the end of his line.*'

Naturally urban Jimmy would despise rural Wordsworth (1770–1850). The poem he refers to ends with the lines 'And then my heart with pleasure fills/And dances with the daffodils.' As Helena offers the olive-branch of 'reasonableness' to Jimmy, Alison unexpectedly comes out with an important truth, and that is that Jimmy *needs* his suffering. Significantly, it is when he begins his attack on Helena that Alison shows signs of crumbling. The idea of church sparks off the memory of his marriage, and he spares nothing to show what he feels it was like. The comparisons of 'slaughter' and 'execution' show how bitterly Jimmy feels about being caught in the conventional domestic trap of marriage. He is speaking out of his own degradation here, and is of course speaking to degrade Alison in compensation.

There is pathos, though, when he turns to her, and indication of his need of her, so often unacknowledged. Helena rouses him again and, ever able to improvise, he links the then leading fashion designer Christian Dior with the proverbial 'wolf in sheep's clothing' in his description of Helena. She represents that fashionable world which he despises for its superficiality and affectations of superiority. The bluntness – 'She is a cow' – contrasts with the pretentiousness, the outwardly so civilized nature of the society he hates. It is only one step to the 'sacred cow' distortion which has so much truth in it. Helena is a wolf, she is predatory, for she has carried off Alison in a sense, and although her standards are hardly to be worshipped ('sacred'), the middle-class superiority she represents often is.

Cliff is put down as Jimmy throws himself into a swingeing attack on financial manipulation: it is based on the fact that those who are 'in the know' always win. It is a long attack even by his standards, and it is ironic that he cites 'Reason and Progress' when his own outburst is irrational. Yet there is an insistence on corrupt financial practices running through the attack. Jimmy feels strongly that the country is swinging back to its old standards, and these mean, as far as he is concerned, the wrong divisions between the haves and have-nots. Underlying this is the further idea that once power has been restored to the 'right' people – and money *is* power – then they will see to it that they are not displaced. The implication is that democracy will be undermined, and any enlightened beliefs will disappear in 'The Big Crash'. Jimmy's fertile mind has cunningly connected the collapse of the stockmarkets on Wall Street in 1929, which brought financial ruin to American big business, with a corresponding economic slump in Europe.

His satire links investment with the self-interest of the future, the idea of storing up security (I use the word deliberately) in the after-life by what amounts to earthly investment. Here Jimmy's attack has a biting edge, connecting religious faith with material wealth. No one can avoid death: it is 'a capital gain, and it's all yours'. Jimmy has been completely carried away by his attack on the capitalist system, its links with religion, and its rooted basis in class.

He switches direction now, attacking Helena in the person of those who are against progress, who shut themselves off, who live in the traditions and cushioned attractions of the past (p. 56). The 'cottage of the soul' suggests a refuge from life experience. Having attacked what he considers the false life, Jimmy now turns to what constitutes real life for him, the suffering attendant upon death. Both Jimmy and Helena are now on the edge of violence: Jimmy is enjoying the idea of breaking the rule that a man never raises his hand to a woman. Helena's rejoinder is to tell him that he is talking nonsense, but Jimmy is further excited by the fact that she is beginning to stand up to him. His recall takes the form of bitterness laced with anger, and his memories have a passionate immediacy, that of the ten-year-old boy watching his father die.

This Spanish Civil War reference carries the telling implication that people then fought for what they believed in: those days are gone. But then Franco's 'god-fearing gentlemen' won. In the recounting of his personal tragedy Jimmy has to be centre stage – he asserts that he was the only person who really cared about his father's suffering. Jimmy's father may well have been thought odd because of his commitment to the Republican cause.

There is a briefly telling comment on Jimmy's parents' marriage. One gets the feeling of divisions here, with the man allying himself to principle while the woman is interested in 'fashionable associations', at least as recorded from her son's viewpoint. It is likely that this family disharmony was a conditioning factor which helps to account for so much of Jimmy's later behaviour. He is intent on proving a point, that people turn their backs on death because of their emotional failure to come to terms with it. We have a sneaking feeling that Jimmy's mother wasn't so bad, but Jimmy is determined to extract the utmost from his own story. This does not make the story any the less moving. The ironic use of the word 'veteran', which is connected with experience in war, shows how deeply Jimmy feels what he says, that as a child he had to suffer without knowing what it was all about. Terms like 'feverish failure' (p. 58) and the use of repetition convey the length of time of his suffering and, more movingly, the length of time it took his father to die. This experience is the crystallizing motive for his anger, the looking back into the past which oppresses and dramatizes so much of his present.

His sudden use of the word 'betrayal' brings us back to that present with a jolt. When Helena exits, Jimmy is able to focus his anger on Alison with the bitter 'What are you trying to do to me?'. His use of the word 'Judas' stresses the betrayal, 'phlegm' being the filthiest thing he can think of by association. Ironically, what has failed to move Alison hitherto now succeeds. The insult seems to be the more effective because of Helena's absence and the fact that it involves her. All the while the audience is aware of the additional strain on Alison, the fact that she is pregnant. But Alison, who only wants peace, has had enough, and Jimmy now turns his attention to Cliff. He tries to involve Cliff in giving an opinion. Then he turns again on Alison as she looks for her gloves, and projects his anger into the future, visualizing her coming back to him, exulting in the extremes of feeling which he envisages. We register the sadism once more – 'grovel' and 'tears' are the operative words.

The cruelty of his distorted vision produces a powerful dramatic effect and, poignantly, it has a terrible flavour of prophecy about it, for Alison does return later, patently ill, suffering, and prepared to grovel. Helena's matter-of-fact announcement of the phone call is further evidence of Osborne's dramatic craftsmanship. Just when we feel that the present scene cannot be sustained much longer at its current temperature, the phone call provides the breathing space. Helena's reaction is typically sadistic too, for she feels physically violent towards Jimmy. By contrast, she is almost maternal towards Alison. Cliff's silence gives way to positive, revealing expression (p. 60). Helena baits him for not standing up to Jimmy, but Cliff has worked out the nature of human relationships, how conflicts and extremes of feeling take over, dominate, and so often wreck those relationships.

We have become used to the imagery of violence and war which appropriately characterizes so much of the play. Here words like 'battlefield' and 'no man's land' and 'very narrow strip of plain hell' underline that atmosphere. Cliff himself emphasizes the class differences: the poorer elements of society often live in domestic strife, whereas the middle classes are supposedly too civilized to do so. His final words where he expresses his love for Jimmy and Alison universalize, terribly and movingly, the human situation: they stress that men and women were born to suffer.

Helena's response is to invoke those middle-class standards by which she lives or thinks she lives. But by sending the telegram to Colonel Redfern she has done what she has all along been threatening to do – taken over Alison *and* her relationship with Jimmy. The truth is that Alison is so battered that her awareness and her resistance are lowered. Helena's use of 'dear' is expressive of their intimacy: her use of 'home' shows that she is determined to put the clock back for Alison. The latter's responses are those of someone completely reduced by circumstances. There is, or appears to be, a moment of doubt in her own mind as to whether she can go through with it. This is shown by the pause before she agrees to go. Helena continues in command, saying that Jimmy may 'come to his senses' after Alison has left, but she has difficulty with the words which perhaps reflect the fact that she doesn't understand her own motives. Has she admitted to herself what she is doing and why? The word 'betrayal' used so often by Jimmy, comes back into our minds here.

Jimmy's entrance and his announcement that Hugh's mum has had a stroke immediately focuses dramatic attention. In a sense, he has unexpectedly got what he has been asking for in others. He has the complete attention of the audience, and for once his verbal and emotional strength has been sapped by the news. He is now exposed and vulnerable, rubbing his fists over his face, presumably to get rid of the traces of tears. He is so overcome by the news that he reacts in a middle-class way by ordering a taxi to be sent for him. He now looks back in sentiment and nostalgia. During the scene we feel the ironic effect. Jimmy does not know that Alison is about to leave him, though Cliff knows and the two women know. Jimmy is not just working himself into a passion, he is genuinely moved. No literary references come to his aid – instead simple language fits his mood, like 'pure gold'. Perhaps subconsciously, a passing echo of a popular song of the period 'She got a kick out of you' also comes into his mind.

The end of the scene is unbearably moving. Firstly, there is Alison handing Jimmy his shoes and kneeling down to do so, which almost suggests her subjection to him. Then there is Jimmy's humble admission of his need for her at this sudden new crisis of his life – this shows him natural, vulnerable, more abject than we have hitherto seen. Again the stage directions tell strongly: the characters have run out of words, but everything else speaks directly to the audience. The ringing of the church bells is symbolic of, prelude to, Alison's leaving him: her going to church with Helena is the simple dramatic equivalent of going out of his life. The picking-up of the prayer-book shows that the decision has been taken – and all this is done in silence, with objects and movements standing for words. The wavering is another fine dramatic touch, the fact that the words when they come are *hardly audible* is another and reflects the emotional strain.

Now comes Jimmy's moving reaction after she has gone. He is rejected. The treatment of the teddy bear, which is of course symbolic of the private fantasy he shares with Alison, shows the anguish and frustration and despair he is undergoing. Osborne's irony – the bear making the sound it is supposed to make (an echo of Jimmy's feelings) – is an unobtrusive dramatic stroke. Admittedly there is a touch of gimmickry about this, yet somehow it echoes Jimmy's own character.

ACT II SCENE ii

This marks the short passage of time until the next evening but is momentous with activity. Colonel Redfern is far from the stereotype we have come to expect. There is an interesting emphasis on his past which gives him points of contact with Jimmy. We notice that he is assessing the situation rather than commenting critically on it. We never meet Mrs Redfern, yet because of Jimmy's 'creation' of her she is a potent presence in the play. The dialogue is quieter; it is what Helena would call decent and civilized, Jimmy sterile and apathetic. Alison fills in details for her father, and his diffidence is seen in the brevity of his replies. He has no knowledge of the world in which Jimmy lives.

There is some humour in the idea of an actor marrying a charwoman, but then there is a certain incongruity, as Colonel Redfern points out, in an 'educated young man' like Jimmy running a sweet-stall. For Jimmy of course the choice was an important one – in working in a market he is being loyal to his working-class roots. Alison lists the other things that he has tried, all of which involve 'selling', whether it is the words of the journalist or advertiser or the practical fact of the vacuum cleaner.

For the Colonel this visit is an eye-opener, but instead of reacting conventionally, he actually thinks that he sees some justice in Jimmy's rejection of him and his kind. The unexpectedness of this admission again increases the dramatic temperature. He further admits that his wife went too far in her past actions, and shows that he will put up with things rather than oppose them. This unstressed connection – like father, like daughter – gives the Colonel credibility. In the same way that the Colonel has been unable to restrain his wife, so Alison has been unable to restrain Jimmy. Before the Colonel goes into his diffident retreat we should note that we are being given insights into his marriage, and that it is being contrasted with that of Alison and Jimmy.

The Colonel has a capacity for self-blame, and sees his wife's actions and Jimmy's as being 'in good faith'. He follows this with his 'sitting on the fence' theory, but Alison will not accept this. Our sympathies are with her, for she certainly had to get off the fence of cosy security in order to marry Jimmy. For a moment here Alison herself looks back in anger: the Colonel, we feel, is looking back with a kind of disillusion, but also with wisdom, not bitterness.

In another ironic stroke Osborne has Colonel Redfern refer to the letters that Alison wrote, the letters which Jimmy regarded as a betrayal. The Colonel is almost blaming Alison here, doubtful, perhaps frightened, of becoming involved in her marriage, which is her problem. Alison quotes what Jimmy has said about her mother and about the Colonel, hoping no doubt that this will rouse him into active condemnation of Jimmy. It doesn't work. His appreciation of Jimmy's 'turn of phrase' is followed by a 'without malice' wish that Alison had never met him. Alison now employs the literary and contemporary references – like Jimmy – to give point to what she is saying. She has already quoted Jimmy's phrase about her mother being 'A good blow-out for the worms' (a first-rate meal), but now she throws in the 'sixty-four dollar question' – the one which had to be answered in the American quiz shows of the period if the contestant was to win the money. Then comes the revenge suggestion and the Shelley, Mary and Godwin reference (p. 67). Shelley, the romantic poet (1792–1822), was a rebel who consistently denounced the corruptions of politics and the aristocratic life, and his wife Mary wrote *Frankenstein* (1818). Her father William was the novelist and philosopher (1756–1836). Alison is demonstrating the difference between this threesome and herself, Jimmy and her father.

She says that only Helena could understand the challenge that

Jimmy poses, and there is certainly irony here in the fact that Helena, whether she chooses to acknowledge it or not, has accepted the 'challenge' of Jimmy. The Colonel's reaction is simple – he believes in love and not the complexities of relationships – and he sees that Alison has learned a lot from Jimmy. The Colonel's own look back shows him displaced in the society to which he has returned. The dates here – 1914 and 1947 – are important, for they mean that the Colonel has missed the First and Second World Wars (1914–18 and 1939–45). He would have felt the impact of the Second World War in India because of the threat of Asian conquest by the Japanese. Apart from his leaves, he would know nothing of the economic depression in England in the 1930s. Nor would he have experienced at first hand the immediate post-war consequences in 1945, one of which was the election of a Labour government in a landslide victory that year.

He is sensitive about his own position and reactions, hence his reference to the 'Blimps'. Colonel Blimp originated as a cartoon character who epitomized the old colonial attitude of pride in the British Empire and an abiding belief in the standards which made it. Hence anything modern was regarded by the Blimps with horror, here expressed in the cliché 'going to the dogs'. We sense that the Colonel's look back contains a buried anger because everything had to change. Just as Jimmy creates a vivid picture of his past so the Colonel creates one of his too, right through to the end of it with the 'dirty little train' and the band playing.

Alison's picking up of the squirrel (p. 68) is an immediate dramatic and poignant gesture which signals change for her, movement away from Jimmy, from conflict, but also away from the treasured fantasy which they share. Notice how important this prop is, like others, in the action of the play. The fact that she does *not* put the squirrel in her suitcase is significant. It can play no part where she is going. By returning it, of course, she may be leaving Jimmy the small comfort of their shared fantasy.

With the entrance of Helena right on cue (p. 68) we are aware that at this point there is no question of going back on what has been decided. It is significant too that Alison has not packed everything, almost as if she is leaving the way clear for a return. She does not say that Cliff can send anything on. There is some feeling in us that Alison does not intend the break to be a final one. The Colonel, anxious to get away, reveals that he has talked his wife out of coming, evidence of his own tact. Now comes the dramatic revelation that Helena is staying, her excuse being that she has an appointment in Birmingham the next day. Almost on her words Cliff enters.

The tension is generated now as the characters adjust to the news, with Alison assuming an affected casualness. But with the Colonel gone, Cliff is quick to reveal his own reading of the situation and that he sees into and through Helena. His 'You'll be here' (p. 70) is the most overt statement of recognition. Helena, he feels, wants to tell Jimmy that Alison has gone: she is also making herself available to him.

Cliff's gesture of putting his arm around Alison shows his sympathetic concern, but he also finds the time to get at Helena, his words implying that she is responsible for the separation of Jimmy and Alison. He does his utmost to reassure Alison when he says 'We'll keep the old nut-house going'. Alison's look around the room is a silent leave-taking of all that she has known. When she goes the focus is entirely on Cliff and Helena. Cliff's mood is seen when he rejects the cup of tea, her tension in the lighting of the cigarette. Cliff is irritated by her mini-interrogation, and his humour now deserts him. At this stage he does not want to be a member of this changed threesome.

Tension builds as we wait for Jimmy's return. Cliff senses that Jimmy will be hurt, and his bitter angry lines before he exits shows that he blames Helena for what has happened. Her movements and actions when she is left alone tell us much about her state of mind and her feelings. There is a certain restlessness about her until she picks up the bear. Her holding it tells us that she has consciously or unconsciously taken over Alison's role in the fantasy: also that she possesses or wishes to possess Jimmy. The latter's entry is as explosive as Cliff's exit (p. 72). Jimmy is looking back in immediate anger, but we feel for him when he reads Alison's letter. Its language is the last straw and certainly 'deep, loving need', while it may reflect Alison's sincerity, is to him a sentimentalized underlining of her inadequacy.

At the height of his anger Helena reveals Alison's secret. And here Osborne shows once again the reality of character in action. Jimmy reacts as we might have expected he would. He doesn't go 'soggy at the knees'; although he registers the news, he is more immediately taken with the positive and unexpected role that Helena is playing. There follows one of the most outrageous diatribes of the play even by Jimmy's standards, but there is little doubt that although he begins quietly he is trying to provoke a reaction in Helena. He appears to be testing her out. He is also getting an emotional release after Alison's letter and after the terrible claustrophobia of seeing Hugh's mother die. While he is craving the extremes of emotion in ordinary life, he is human enough to be made bitter and angry when he sees suffering in another. Alison has contributed to his mood by not even sending flowers.

Jimmy reaches a crescendo, and that crescendo is a breaking point. His 'I can't believe it' conveys the totality of his anguish. He turns on Helena, but she responds in a way that he isn't used to (p. 73). The *slap* is the release of her feelings, just as he has been releasing his in reaction. It is an indication of the passion that she feels for him, and the disbelief he registers shows his surprise at the response and his bewilderment at the feelings which have occasioned it. The despair is perhaps at the inevitability he now faces – a conflict with Helena to follow the conflict with Alison. But Helena knows now what she wants. The suddenness of her action – she is following her friend Alison in her quest for experience in that other world which is Jimmy's – provides the perfect dramatic climax to the act.

ACT III SCENE i

Helena has replaced Alison in the threesome, but the atmosphere, the setting and the situation are a deliberate re-creation of the first scene in the play. The duplication is there right down to the detail of Helena wearing Jimmy's shirt, but of course there are differences which stress Helena's individuality. The *déjà vu* (the feeling of having been somewhere before, or of having enacted the same situation before) element is very strong. It exercises a fascinating effect on audience and reader alike. What has changed?

The idea of 'pictures' of sexual fertility rites would have been enough to boost sales in the much less permissive period in which Osborne is writing. The fascination of the public for black magic and satanic rituals was particularly strong in the 1950s: Jimmy would naturally seize upon the association of the débutante and Market Harborough, since it reflects the (supposed) degraded practices of the upper reaches of society. Jimmy quickly goes up-market in his reference to Fortnum's, the fashionable and prestigious West End store of Fortnum and Mason. The use of the word 'workout', another boxing association, implies that Miss Drury has to be in training, or is rehearsing her evil practices. The tone is typical of the Jimmy we have come to know, and perhaps to loathe, in Act I, but Helena's response, brief though it is, is very different from what Alison's would have been. She jokes with Jimmy on the same level.

Then he adopts the cliché-ridden working-class language of the area, a parody here of non-communication. Osborne's ear for such nuances is excellent, the commonplaces reflecting the meaningless exchanges of everyday life. Jimmy soon reverts to black magic and Alison's mother, mentioning that other superior West End store, Harrods. Although Helena humours him, he manages to get in a dig at the nature of religious or superstitious sacrifice – 'you give up something you never really wanted in the first place'.

This leads to a general attack on the social/moral level, the image that people project of themselves when they wish to be seen giving up something. He reverses the generally accepted code by saying that we should feel sorry for those who give up something. He moves easily into his anti-establishment vein: Helena would naturally have 'blue' blood, and this he wittily associates with Cambridge, which represents something of an establishment monopoly, that of the aristocratic public school tradition. 'The Coptic Goddess of Fertility' is an imaginative leap, for the Copts, natives of Egypt, were converted to Christianity. It would appear that the implications are that pagan rites and worship of the Virgin Mary have been conveniently connected by Jimmy. Cliff's response and Jimmy's affected elevation of it produce a genuine comic flavour, the pattern of the play's first scene being continued here. Jimmy throws in another topical reference of a controversial nature, that to 'artificial insemination'.

His next 'send-up', a distortion of course, is of scholarly speculation about the irrelevant biographical details in the lives of great men ('whether Milton wore braces or not'). The term 'shot down' (as in battles between aircraft) is a hangover from the war. This cliché-type comment is continued by Cliff ('bitten the dust', 'going up in flames'). Obviously the cliché-type language is meant as an ironic comment on the elevated nothingness of the controversy, where learned language which did not mean anything might be employed on either side of the debate. All Souls, the Oxford College, is another establishment focal point, because it is an academic hierarchy, while the Athenaeum, a prestigious London club, has similar associations with leisured power and status.

Having been condescending to Cliff, Jimmy keeps up his anti-intellectual attacks. The Shakespeare sequence wittily embraces the academic craze to discover something new, particularly about Shakespeare, where so little is known, and to link it with whatever is sensational, so that it will have a popular as well as an academic appeal. The 'second best bed' reference (p. 78) is what Shakespeare left to his wife. Helena at least appreciates the humour, crude though it is, especially its picking up of homosexual associations with Shakespeare. But she is hurt by the mention of sin.

Cliff is aware of the danger signs, and Jimmy continues to bait Helena through the religion/church remarks; his rendering of 'muscular Christianity' is 'spiritual beefcake', a sarcastic comment on spiritual strength which is aggressive in its assertion of what is right. At the same time there is a self-mocking tone, for Jimmy is thin, weedy, and certainly not 'beefcake'. He is mocking the contemporary advertising of body-building, the claim to be able to transform a weakling through exercise into a fine physical specimen of manhood. 'I was a liberal skinny weakling' is a deliberate echo of the words of such an advertisement, with 'liberal' added in of course in Jimmy's inimitable manner. The irony is in the last sentence ('passion of kindliness'), where the impersonality or inadequacy of the church or faith on a personal level is stressed.

The mockery continues: 'more uplift than a starlet' is a crude joke, bosoms at the time being enhanced by firmly-supportive bras. But Jimmy allows himself to be led into the music-hall routine with Cliff which he loves so much. He employs his usual grotesque humour in the choice of the song-title. Helena is quick to encourage this change of mood. 'Jock and Day' (p. 79) is brilliantly punned into 'jocund', while the quotation from *Romeo and Juliet* is soon discarded as being too intellectual. The remarks about Harvard and Yale (the American equivalents of Oxford and Cambridge) show Jimmy looking back to his exploitation of the Shakespeare-changed-his-sex theory. Although he has reprimanded himself for being too intellectual he now introduces another literary association, fantasizing that their act might be called after the author of *The Waste Land* (see p. 21) and the 'mountainous sports girl' of John Betjeman's poem 'Pot Pourri from a Surrey Garden'. Cliff in response parodies a compère or announcer, and they go into their routine at great speed. This is the stand-up music-hall comedian's act of the period, the 'quips' are fast and furious, the word-play obvious and corny but effective. And it would be spoken in the comic and affected manner of the period. The joke on Little Gidding (the title of one of T. S. Eliot's *Four Quartets*) with the pun on 'gelding iron' (an instrument for castrating) merely serves to underline the running associations in Jimmy's mind.

Notice the cunning variation here of the situation in Act I. Then Alison hurt her arm, here Helena, much tougher than Alison physically and emotionally, is unscathed by the routine. Appropriately, the manner of the two great comedians of the day, Bud Flanagan and Chesney Allen, is used, including the song-and-dance finale for which they were celebrated. Osborne here puts together a pastiche of popular-song clichés, but they are inlaid with satirical suggestion (p. 81). There is the mention of Roedean, the expensive and prestigious girls' public school, associated in Jimmy's mind with Helena and Alison. The 'certain little lady' could refer to either of the girls, while 'mother' and 'dad' and their views mirror Jimmy's feelings about Alison's parents. The other lyrical echoes here, so sentimental and typical of the period, contrast with the reality of the apartment: the rest of the song is a self-conscious expression of Jimmy's own situation and his class hang-ups. We note that part of the technique here is to fiddle with the rhyme; the crude one, unacceptable at the time, for 'classes' is 'arses', but the innocuous 'noses' is deliberately substituted. The interjection 'They call me Sydney' is a deliberate use of a Flanagan and Allen technique, the introduction of an irrelevant line, a kind of pause, in a sentimental ballad.

The proposed washing of Cliff's shirt finds him uncertain whether to accept. Jimmy urges him to: Cliff appears to give in for Jimmy's sake, since this involves his acceptance of Helena. Jimmy indulges his sarcasm at Cliff's expense, for now he has no shirt on he can be compared with the current 'beefcake' of American films, Marlon Brando, star of *A Streetcar Named Desire* (1951). But Cliff is on edge, still looking back with nostalgia to the time when Alison was there. He faces Jimmy with the uncomfortable home-truth that at one time he (Jimmy) did not like Helena. Jimmy responds crudely with the degrading analogy between a woman and a meal, the indulgence of appetite.

Cliff now announces that he is thinking of moving out, and again the dramatic temperature changes. He is trying to appear considerate by saying that Helena has too much to do, extending this by adding that he must find a girl for himself anyway. The use of 'dear boy' and 'chaps' is a give-away: this middle-class jargon, which neither of them uses naturally, shows that Cliff and Jimmy are on edge. Jimmy responds directly, then fantasizes about Cliff marrying and being made clean and respectable (p. 84). The jokes are overtaken by Jimmy's real feelings, the fact that he values Cliff more than 'half a dozen Helenas', as he puts it. This, typically, underlines his fear of women – they devour him just as a little madam will devour Cliff. The latter's simple 'Right' is expressive of their tie to each other.

Jimmy now focuses his bitterness on the current blood-donor campaign, and his reference to the good cause harks back to the 'good' cause of the Spanish Civil War, with which he identifies very strongly on his father's account. Jimmy is anti atom-bomb and nuclear war, cynically observing that we shall all be wiped out if it comes, and there will be a 'Brave New – nothing' (p. 85). Here he can't resist the literary association with Aldous Huxley's *Brave New World* (1932), the futuristic novel in which scientific achievements are used to determine class, ability, social occupation, etc., with the elimination of human suffering and emotion as we know it.

With Helena's re-entrance there is another shift of dramatic focus, and Jimmy shifts his role by expressing concern at seeing her behind the ironing-board. We remember that he didn't bother to make this kind of comment with Alison. Then he adopts the pseudo-tough tone of the American film hero of the period, using the standard clichés 'glammed up' and 'hit the town', terms hardly appropriate to the Midland scene. Jimmy is hurt underneath by the fact that Cliff told Helena before he told him that he was going to leave. He concentrates though on praising Cliff for his 'big heart', his generosity of spirit.

His give-and-take appraisal of Cliff is now transferred to Helena as he accepts that she is the one who is giving, who apparently expects nothing from their relationship except for what they give one another in the present. Again the imagery of war is invoked to exemplify conflict and passion yet he implies that he is tired of fighting, not just her but his past and the hatefulness and apathy of the present. Although they 'embrace fiercely' we feel the desperation of his words, 'Don't let anything go wrong'. There is in this plea something of the child crying out for reassurance and protection from the depths of his insecurity. Neither Helena nor Jimmy appears to have thought through the situation.

Alison's return changes everything. It is a dramatic masterstroke, for she has been, I suggest, completely forgotten, by us as well as by Jimmy and Helena. Jimmy's response after the *stunned pause* seems to be calculatedly cynical. It is a finely contrived ending to the scene. The two women, who have never been in overt conflict, are left facing each other, the one conscious of her possession of the other's man, the other bowed down by life and, as we are soon to learn, by death.

ACT III SCENE ii

The stage directions make it clear that neither of the women can escape from the influence of Jimmy. The trumpet punctuates what they are saying anyway. Alison's picking up the pipe and scooping up the ash is a simple reflex action, but poignant because of its associations – she obviously wants her life with Jimmy back. Her account of her compulsion to come is moving, full of personal drama and self-blame, but understandable and convincing. To speak of her sense of timing as being 'in very bad taste' is to utter words which she and Helena would understand in their past, but it does not explain at all her present motivation. Her suffering is seen in her disconnected statements, the idea of being 'Suspended and rather remote' and the praise for the cup of tea. Helena soon reveals her innate, conventional, moral sense. She asserts the rights of the wife, and when Alison criticizes her conventional approach ('the book of rules') Helena is quick to reveal that despite her passion for Jimmy she has never been able to forget that he is married. Alison, with a Jimmy-like facility of association, invokes 'the divine rights of marriage'.

Alison continues to justify herself for coming, still employing the stale middle-class phrases from which she cannot escape. But when we learn what has happened we suspect that her own word, 'hysteria', best explains the state she is in. We feel that for Helena Alison's return has come as something of a relief. By not taxing her with betrayal, by not being outraged, Alison has succeeded in making her feel *ashamed*, where words might only have provoked anger. The simple stage direction *She leans back* . . . clearly indicates the divisions in Helena. She recognizes that Alison has been so influenced by Jimmy that 'You sound as though you were quoting him all the time' (p. 89).

The contrast is now made very clear. Alison says that she did not believe in Helena's way of life: Helena's response shows her class and moral loyalties. Again Osborne employs the 'look back' technique to fill in the gaps: we learn that Helena had written to Alison to tell her that she loved Jimmy, something that Alison found hard to accept. We feel that Helena's extreme reactions against Jimmy when she first came were an attempt to counteract her own strong sexual feelings for him. The scene is a kind of confessional for each of the women: they conclude that Jimmy 'was born out of his time' (p. 90). Helena applies her own standards and expectations to him, the standards of a society which he despises.

Helena too has been influenced by Jimmy's manner and method. Her reference to the French Revolution (1789) which saw the overturning of a decadent monarchy and continued with terrible extremes of violence and brutality, is just what Jimmy would appreciate – that was one of the 'good brave causes' he referred to earlier. The strong suggestion is that Jimmy will carry on just as he is, objecting to everything, warring with the establishment. Alison's reply, her literary reference to Lytton Strachey's *Eminent Victorians* (1918) is at first sight puzzling. These biographical essays about famous people in that period certainly stressed their causes and achievements in the author's own highly individual style. Alison's tone is ironic: Jimmy could never be 'eminent'. Helena now condemns herself (p. 90), and we sense her relief that her confession is out.

Alison now sees Jimmy as deserted (betrayed?) if Helena goes, though Helena believes that she knows how Jimmy will react. Her analogy with the Renaissance popes, who were materialistic and indulged the sins of the flesh, is a deliberately insulting distortion. But the reason for Helena's guilt comes sharply into focus when we learn that Alison has lost her baby (p. 91). Helena's simple, conventional and religious interpretation of this is 'It's like a judgement on us'. Alison, though inwardly in a tumult of emotion herself, is much the more rational and down-to-earth of the two in her acceptance of what has happened. But the trumpet is never silent: it is as if Jimmy is speaking to each of the women in his own way.

Literary references continue. The mother–courtesan association is clear, but the Cleopatra–Boswell one is more obscure. Cleopatra was the legendary Queen of Egypt who seduced the Roman leaders sent to subdue her, chief among them Mark Antony. She represents the licentious sexuality which Alison feels Jimmy needs. Boswell (1740–95) recorded everything he could about the great man of letters of the eighteenth century Samuel Johnson (1709–84). Perhaps the implication is that Jimmy needs a woman who will be sensitive to all his actions and needs. Meanwhile, Alison is fearful that Jimmy has rejected her and doesn't want to see her.

When Jimmy enters we feel that his indifference is feigned: he knows intuitively about the death of the baby. The tension is generated by the silent suffering of Alison and the maternally comforting role that Helena is adopting towards her. Jimmy goes quiet, but claims his share of the suffering: he can't be left out of anything emotional. It is Alison's first loss, and in a sense we feel that she and Jimmy are beginning to move towards one another through their suffering. There remains the terrible irony that Jimmy had said that he wanted this to happen. He refers to Alison as 'her'. Helena is moved to positive action, taking Jimmy's hand (she is still divided against herself) and insists that Alison is not to blame for anything that has happened. With commendable directness Helena announces her decision. We might expect a tirade, but we get silence: it is broken by Helena's passion, love, her inability to go on hurting 'someone else'. Jimmy does not rise to the bait: he merely accepts. Helena is deflated but busies herself with Alison's needs.

Jimmy's reaction sets in with a vengeance. We have heard his 'pain of life' theme before. He indicts Helena for her inability to cope with suffering in life. While he is talking he is really seeing her on her way by gathering up all her things. His irony is seen throughout, particularly when he puts the dress into the arms of the potential 'saint'. But he is shaken by the unprepared finality of the parting. The bells now provide the noise background to the action again, with Alison silent and Jimmy attacking her, here about not sending flowers to Hugh's mother's funeral. Soon he is sounding out the nature of their conflict: he is led towards the familiar imagery of the bear (their fantasy) before he looks back to the first sight of Alison at the party. He sounds a note that goes some way to explaining conflict between people, the fact that what we think we see – *appearance* – is sometimes the very reverse of what is – *reality*. Alison's 'wonderful relaxation of spirit' (p. 94) is what Jimmy wants, but perhaps the real relaxation does not come until one has lived and suffered.

Now there is the telling reality of Alison's own suffering. Her outburst is a mixture of anguish, of self-dramatics, of the wish to get Jimmy back at all costs, and of self-recognition. 'I want to be corrupt and futile' shows her desperation. Jimmy looks on *helplessly*, the italicized word being picked up and articulated in Alison's 'that helpless human being inside my body'. We remember Jimmy's frightening attacks on Alison, how he had accused her of devouring him, and how too he had said that he was inside her stomach. This connects Jimmy and the baby, both helpless, both in need of Alison, and both 'lost causes'. Alison obviously feels that she has failed Jimmy and the baby.

Her death-wish brings her closer to Jimmy, since it represents the extreme of suffering: you have to bleed emotionally; and she is brought closer when she admits 'all I could think of was you and what I'd lost'. This, then, is what has moved her to return: in the most poignant of all senses Jimmy has proved to be right. You need to live and to *feel* in order to be certain of your own identity. For once Alison is absolutely centre stage. This self-revelation is moving, even degrading in terms of Alison's self-abasement, as the play moves towards their coming together on the terms that Jimmy has said he wants, and which Alison has met. The souls in Hell and torment reference shows that Alison is at the end of her tether. She can have no more children: Jimmy has got all that he asked for and more. We feel disgust, despair: Osborne is facing us with reality, terrible reality – our own reality: there is no holding back.

With Alison's collapse and Jimmy's taking her in his arms a different note is sounded, and the poignancy of the ending is as unbearable as anything that has preceded it. Jimmy is silent, itself unusual, and expressive here too of his feelings. His fragments of speech convey his inability to take the emotional pressure that is now being thrust upon him. There is the retreat from life to the world of fantasy they have built. Now it is the often abrasive Jimmy's turn to be comforting and consoling, to treat Alison as if she is a child, to take the two of them, 'lost causes', away from the life that has proved too much for them. There is pathos in what Jimmy says, particularly in its defenceless animal associations. Thus retreat, with honey, nuts, warmth, caves, suggests security, but it also suggests the kind of isolation needed to sustain love. The 'soppy, scruffy sort of bear' (all too often with a sore head) is the Jimmy who knows himself: 'helping to keep my claws in order' is a sad plea to Alison to make him conform. The fantasy here becomes the symbol of reduction, the escape which has a deeper pathos underlining it, that of eventual acceptance of what has to be. The 'traps' will always be there to maim and kill the 'rather mad, slightly satanic, and very timid little animals'. Alison, 'none too bright', is liable to be hurt, while Jimmy is aware of what his own attitudes must be like to others. The simple emphasis is on their need for each other. In a strangely ironic way the ending is happy, but it is mock-happy really. If we accept the reality of Jimmy and Alison, then we have also to accept that conflicts will continue: but they have each other, a degree of self-recognition, knowledge of who they are and what they want.

The Characters

JIMMY PORTER

It will be obvious to any reader or audience of *Look Back in Anger* that Jimmy Porter dominates the action and that he is meant to do so. The description of him at the beginning of the play is important to an understanding of his character and personality. The 'worn tweed jacket and flannels' indicate a disregard of appearance, a determined assertion of rebellion against the conventions of dressing smartly or well. Even the pipe is a mark of independence: others have to put up with the smoke. Osborne's choice of language to describe him is particularly vivid, for it gives the essential ingredients of Jimmy's personality and the contradictions inherent in it. Most important is the fact that Jimmy is a *dramatic* character, a stage presence almost before a word is spoken. There is nothing negative about Jimmy: all is positive, calculated to offend or provoke those with whom he is in interaction: the audience will sit up and respond directly he begins to speak. Remember that they will not know of the stage directions, but that the director and producer will have them constantly in mind as the actor who plays Jimmy develops the character. As readers we might ponder on the use of a word like 'freebooting': you might also consider the implications of 'Blistering honesty, or apparent honesty', and see which of these emphases applies most accurately to Jimmy in your view as his character unfolds. Jimmy is abrasive, argumentative, finding fault with what he reads, insulting to Cliff and to Alison. His hang-ups about class are soon apparent and he is never (until the end of the play at least) at a loss for words. He is loud and aggressive, yet we are aware that this masks intense feelings of insecurity. His outward behaviour is often offensive, particularly towards Alison, whose background and lack of direct or positive response to what he says combine to exasperate him. This often leads him on to a liberty of insult. Despite this, there is a strong feeling of attraction between them: a simple stage direction like *His eyes meet hers* (p. 13) conveying their sexual intimacy and Jimmy's feelings for her.

He can be potently sarcastic, but we are aware of what he doesn't say, perhaps because he cannot bring himself to say them, words of tenderness or regret. His comments, frequently on current events, fail to elicit the positive response that he requires: it irks Jimmy greatly that they fail to do so. He longs for 'a little ordinary human enthusiasm', and his irony is directed easily at the other two when he suggests that they pretend to be 'human beings'. He is easily provoked by the non-responses, seeing Alison's low-key replies as the ultimate in apathy, maintaining that she would learn to accept anything. The ruthless quality in Jimmy which was indicated in the stage directions becomes increasingly apparent. At the beginning, on a dull Sunday, he is casting around for something to do. It is quite clear that he will not settle to anything, while his regret for the past shows the rootlessness of the present as far as he is concerned. Part of that past contained his affair with Madeline. It is an important index to Jimmy's character, for he is vulnerable, needs mothering (this partly explains Helena's feeling of attraction towards him). Madeline, the older woman, temporarily provided the security he needs.

Jimmy has graduated from a red-brick university, and it is clear that he does not know where he belongs in society. The sweet-stall is working-class work, but his education has raised his cultural level: he is in a no man's land between idealism and rejection. He finds that his rebellious and anti-establishment comments enable him to use his acquired cultural associations – literature, music, art – while his range of contemporary political reference is a wide one. He is determinedly against the American Age, despising the materialistic pseudo-civilization with its macho and synthetic sexual images. Always he returns to Alison's family: he ridicules brother Nigel, the upwardly-mobile politician, and Mummy and Daddy, those entrenched middle-class standard-bearers. They will always provide him with an opportunity to exercise his rhetoric and his wit: Nigel is 'The Platitude from Outer Space' who deserves to be decorated 'For Vaguery in the Field'.

Jimmy is a mimic, particularly when it comes to taking off the Southern England middle-class accents he loathes (he can do Midland accents too). He also indulges in male immature horseplay with Cliff which leads to Alison being hurt: before that there is his marvellously inventive play on the word 'pusillanimous'. Even when he turns the radio on for the music his restlessness is still apparent: irritable as ever, he complains about the interference from the iron. This is followed by a very revealing attack on women: he appears to be frightened of being possessed, of losing his identity in the personality of a partner. There is sometimes a sadistic vehemence about his attack, an attempt to diminish Alison: Jimmy's language of war perhaps reflects his own conflict, the war against women, the fear of being defeated by having to conform. After Alison is hurt by the horseplay Jimmy appears to be genuinely repentant. This shows how quickly his mood changes, from the irresponsible to the aware, from abrasive aggression to quiet regret. When he comes back into the room after the sympathetic exchange between Cliff and Alison, we can see that he needs to re-establish himself, that he has to see himself as the centre of activity within the relationship, whether in a jocular or an aggressive way. We note how quickly he takes over again. This reflects his volatile nature, but it also shows that Alison and Cliff accept him for what he is, even though it means that he may attack them again. After the kidding comes the reckoning. Once Cliff has been despatched to get the cigarettes, Jimmy confesses his guilt in hurting Alison. He also shows just how much he wants her and needs her sexually. He is here sympathetic, almost tender, but we realize how dependent he is not only on Alison but on Cliff. His recognition of Cliff as his only friend is moving, deeply pathetic: inside he is lonely, needing the comfort and reassurance of Cliff and Alison.

Jimmy's unpredictability is against him, for we note that even as Alison strokes his head, she is *still on guard a little*. Alison's confiding in Cliff shows that she cannot rely on a sympathetic response from Jimmy. But once set in a particular direction, Jimmy tends to follow it through. For instance, when his thoughts turn to Hugh's mum, he says what she has done for them, and how inadequate Alison's response to her has been. That way lies further conflict. And he needs the area of fantasy with the bears and the squirrels because he does not find peace and security in the society in which he lives. That escape, first sounded by him and by Alison at the end of the first act, is short-lived, for with the news of Helena's phone call Jimmy is moved to express an extreme aversion for her, even using Helena as an excuse for a further verbal onslaught on women. He expresses the wish – only a passing humour – that he was homosexual – 'they do seem to have a cause'.

There is an unscrupulous side to Jimmy's nature, as we see when he goes through Alison's handbag, telling Cliff that he wants 'to know if I'm being betrayed'. This obsession soon translates itself with unconcealed anger to another attack on Mummy and Daddy, and a further extension of his class hatred of them and what they represent. Jimmy, here at his worst, goes over the top, venting anger, hate, frustration and then a violently sadistic impulse in which he wishes that Alison might have a child and that it should die. The language here reflects the degree of his passion: he has wound himself up in order to provoke a response, but the fear beneath the savagery is shown in the use of the 'python' image. What he seems to fear is that his own sexuality will be lost in Alison's. The wider implications are that he fears being taken over by the wider demands of the woman, and forced into the conventional life which he hates and rejects. It is extreme, sadistic, thoroughly selfish – the last word he uses (and perhaps the first word he thinks of) is 'me'.

With the arrival and quick settling in of Helena we get, as we should expect, a very positive response from Jimmy. Notice that in moments of crisis or of emotional tension Jimmy is able to release some of his pent-up feelings by playing the trumpet. This is a dramatic reminder that he is still present and that at any moment he may re-enter and cause his usual chaos. Helena provokes Jimmy merely by being what she is or, more correctly, what she appears. Much of what we learn about Jimmy in the first scene of the second act comes from Alison's account of him, of how they met and married, to Helena. She tells us that his loyalties are deep ones. The 'question of allegiances' obviously embraces Cliff, Hugh, Hugh's mum, his father in the past as well as 'the other women he loved'. The insights we are given demonstrate this possessive loyalty about the past, even to the pathetic hope that his best friend Hugh would get on with Alison. Perhaps too this shows a certain *naïveté* in Jimmy as well as his need for security in his relationships. When Hugh and Alison do not hit it off together, Jimmy becomes bitter and upset: Alison says that he and Hugh regarded her as a hostage from that very middle-class society which they loathe.

There is much more to it than this, as readers and audience of the play will realize. Hugh initially was playing the role that Cliff has during the play: Jimmy, with another man present, feels protected from Alison, from being possessed by a woman. We note too that in that past the presence of Hugh was an encouragement for Jimmy to indulge in anti-social horseplay. It took the form of gate-crashing parties, whereas later with Cliff, as we have seen, it is a kind of domesticated rough-and-tumble. If we take Alison's word for it, Jimmy is also a sexual opportunist: he unsuccessfully tries to seduce a girl at a party. Alison's early account of Jimmy stresses that he is 'young and frail' and has 'tired lines' around the mouth. This establishes Jimmy's vulnerability and his capacity for suffering. He is impetuous and obstinate, as we see from his quickly becoming determined to marry Alison. It is almost as if by so doing he is taking on, or at least making a gesture against, the establishment he hates. Alison also describes him being 'full of fire'. This implies resolution, courage, passion, the last two certainly being evident in Jimmy's dramatic presence on stage, though they are more verbal than anything else. The break-up between Jimmy and Hugh also presents us with an interesting sidelight on Jimmy's character. Jimmy decides to stay (another indication of his resolution), but there is little doubt that part of his bitterness towards Alison derives from the loss – the 'betrayal' (?) of Hugh. Jimmy's staying is an acknowledgement of Alison's claims on him, but it is also evidence of his own loyalty to her. In a way this is almost conventional, something he would not appreciate. There is also this to consider: Jimmy would know that he has in effect been captured by a woman and that he has lost his friend in the process. Alison herself believes that Jimmy blames her for it (as does Hugh's mother) though he hasn't actually said so.

Jimmy mocks the middle classes he hates by aping their manners – he offers the teapot to Helena and then pours tea out for her. This is an outwardly conforming prelude to his satirical parody of a pop-song (p. 50). Here he is criticizing through the words the nature of a pointless and promiscuous existence. They also repeat his fear of women and contain too a moral tone, a weariness and rejection of a wasted way of life. He follows this with references to Dante and T. S. Eliot (perhaps displaying his 'education'). There is some truth obviously in Helena's accusing him of trying 'so hard to be unpleasant'.

For Jimmy this domestic scene is the means and the excuse to expend his verbal and imaginative powers in rhetorical denunciation. He derives pleasure from this baiting and also from the limited response he gets from Helena: in fact her use of the word 'tiresome' draws forth from Jimmy the most natural and impulsive laughter. It is short-lived, for he rises to anger with the church-going announcement: his rage mounts, he is quick to see a struggle between himself and Helena for Alison. For him, it is inevitably a class struggle.

His next attack on Mummy is as always predictable, but the extremes of the language are obviously undertaken in order to shock Helena. A good example of this is 'She's as rough as a night in a Bombay brothel' and his actions (see brief stage directions p. 52) fittingly reflect his mood. During his attack on Mummy he reveals that she disliked his long hair, but he also shows some self-consciousness about his own appearance, some self-recognition of the image he presents. Here his attempts to provoke Alison are seen in his assertion that she should be dead. He is 'savage' with Cliff, who tries to restrain him.

We notice that running beneath all this is a considered plan of campaign: Jimmy *is* angry but there is some degree of affected feeling too, so that when we are told *He's saving his strength for the knock-out* we see the method underlining the frenzy. The knock-out is intended to break Alison here and now, but Jimmy is surprised by the 'thrust' that she gets home on him, the assertion that he would be lost without his suffering. It is an important insight, an important aspect of Jimmy's character. Here Jimmy lets it pass (though he doubtless stores it for later retrieval) and concentrates on tactics, choosing to address Helena's back.

He shows remarkable mobility of mind and body here in the small space of the flat. His personal probing goes on, pushed by his desire to draw blood, and his account of the marriage is farcical, angry, bitter, and almost certainly distorted ('I remember being sick in the vestry') by his incredible fluency. This is followed by the direct insult, the slow, calculated 'sacred cow' which is levelled at Helena. After this we are told that *His imagination is racing, and the words pour out* (p. 55).

This simple stage direction is the index to Jimmy's dramatic personality: once his imagination is stimulated it takes off, and here he is able to focus on two of his pet hates, religion and big business. He links both together scathingly. Jimmy pushes himself so hard that he comes near to violence, but in his attack he is moving physically and emotionally closer to Helena. With one of those sudden changes which are typical of Jimmy he moves from confrontation to terrible reminiscence. He looks back in anger and anguish to the time when he watched his father die. We now feel that we are seeing into the heart of Jimmy's character, that this was an important time in his life and that it influenced much of his later behaviour. The conditioning of that past has eaten into the present. The small, frightened, bewildered, angry, helpless little boy – all these words are in Jimmy's account – is still very much a part of the outwardly grown man. Jimmy is volatile, and the account is more than tinged with self-pity. But it also shows another side to Jimmy, his capacity to feel for others in the adversity of their pain and suffering. Whatever Jimmy is he has the quality of compassion. This may seem at variance with his treatment of Alison and his insulting of Helena, but these contradictions are present in all of us. Osborne records extremes of feeling and action with deadly accuracy and complete naturalness. Jimmy is recognizably one of us. He is roused into present anger (*disabled rage* Osborne calls it) by Alison's 'betrayal' in going to church. Jimmy always demands attention, and when he doesn't get it he is moved to irrational anger. He is so angry that he is nearly inarticulate. But not quite.

As if anticipating Alison's greater betrayal of really leaving him, he launches into a tirade about the pleasure he will experience at her grovelling return. This is prophetic of what later happens. It shows Jimmy pushing his *supposed* sadism to an extreme, but it is a verbal sadism rather than a physical one, the kind of thing that is said in a moment of over-the-top anger. This terrible sequence is followed, on his return, by an abject, almost broken need of Alison. We feel that despite all his bravado, the 'little boy' of the past is now present, and that he will be unable to cope with the crisis of Hugh's mother. There is something deeply pathetic in Jimmy's broken 'I . . . need you . . . to come with me' and his picking up of the teddy bear and throwing it away – tenderness followed by anger – is typical of him. When he buries his face in the bedclothes we may feel that this is melodramatic self-indulgence. It is. It is also an indication of his suffering and his vulnerability. Jimmy, we feel, cannot bear to be alone, hence his emphasis on the word 'betrayal' which means, in effect, that any rejection of his views and his needs is a rejection of him.

Jimmy is absent from the action of Act II Scene ii in the flesh but not in the spirit. This is because Alison and Colonel Redfern talk about him most of the time. This tends to make his re-entry when it comes all the more effective. He feels (a common state with Jimmy) ill-used, and his reaction to Alison's letter is what we should expect. Knowing how volatile he is Cliff, leaving the house, avoids him. The stage directions here show Jimmy as being *giddy with anger*, which seems to be more than just a reflex response to being nearly knocked down by Daddy. It is occasioned by seeing Alison in the car with him. He must be bewildered, we feel, by seeing Helena *her head back on the pillow still holding the bear*. His 'What's the matter with everybody?' is completely natural in view of the sudden turn of events: his reception of the letter as being a 'polite, emotional mess' is completely in character. His needs would find such a communication inadequate, for it shows his wife's usage of the kind of convention observed by her class and hated by Jimmy. For Jimmy it represents not only betrayal but defeat: his own standards and prescriptions have had so little effect that she has returned to her earlier ways.

Pushed back, Jimmy rejects Alison, perhaps because she has rejected him, and this is seen in his reaction to the news that she is going to have a baby. He switches on quickly to Helena, contemplating her calmness and acceptance, assessing the certainty that she is still there. Although he attacks, we feel that the ferocity he uses indicates his own passion, newly awakened by the situation, for her.

Once again the starting point is his looking back in anger – anger at the suffering of Hugh's mother, anger at the attitude and decision of Alison, anger at himself perhaps in his own boiling frustration and inadequacy. But here – and remember that he accused Alison of being 'phoney', of performing – so he is here performing himself, caught in this grip of anger, moving towards the climax of Helena's expulsion.

Yet his emphasis is in itself a give-away. When he calls her an 'evil-minded little virgin' he is expressing his wish to subdue her, to violate her, to take her *because* she has stood up to him. I am not suggesting that Jimmy knows consciously what he wants: I am saying that he is driven onwards by a mixture of his own anger *and* the need to act the part he has willed himself to play. Very significantly, the slap from

Helena does not call forth the response he had once threatened it would: she has penetrated by her action the outer covering of the little boy still present in Jimmy. His pain and despair must now be assuaged, comforted, by her responsive passion, sexual and maternal at the same time.

In the last act Helena has replaced Alison, but initially there seems to be little change in Jimmy. His mood is similar to that at the beginning of the play, though there are slight variants: Jimmy is still abusing the same emphases in the Sunday papers, but he shows much more consideration towards Helena than he did to Alison earlier. For example, he asks Helena if she is bothered by his pipe-smoking. Admittedly, his attack on the sensational cases of demoniac practices as reported in the press also embraces Helena, though we feel the tone is jocularly ironic rather than serious or unpleasant. His eye is never far from the past (and he may be looking sideways at the present too) and Alison's mother comes in for her usual share of the verbal vitriol. Jimmy also broods about people making sacrifices, contending that when most people give up something it turns out that they didn't really want it anyway.

Jimmy always ranges wherever he wants to go, attacking academic narrowness and obsession, switching to attack Helena's religion, deliberately baiting her by underlining his own lack of spiritual commitment, drawing a clever analogy with physical strength, punning and quoting and plunging into his knockabout music-hall act with Cliff. We always feel that Jimmy needs to perform, however small the audience: it is a necessary part of his search for reassurance. The quick-fire act with Cliff shows him in his favourite role of comedian on his own small stage. In a sense, this too is a fantasy which has some points of contact with that other escape into the world of squirrels and bears. And just as he has to return to reality from that, so he gets tired of the brittle humour of this act, pushing Cliff away when he has had enough. But while Helena sees to Cliff's shirt the two men are left alone: Jimmy, as we should expect, is anxious that Cliff and Helena should get on together. He affects to accept Cliff's decision to leave, but not without revealing his own warm feelings towards him. This shows the consistency with which Osborne presents his character: this situation is similar to the off-stage one with Hugh. Jimmy's fear of women is seen in comic key in his mock-projection that Cliff will succumb and be cleaned up by 'some respectable little madam'. All this kidding is cover for his sense of loss and his fear of being deserted ('betrayed'). His remark to himself that he is always saying goodbye is infinitely pathetic. He switches quickly again, however, to explain his own reactions for Cliff's benefit. This is his admission that he is sexually drawn to Helena, but that although he is prepared to see Cliff go out of his life, he is aware of Cliff's worth both to himself and to others. Jimmy in his way is showing his own brand of loyalty to Cliff here, but he is showing himself too, for Cliff does not make the demands on him that Helena (or any woman for that matter) will. It leads to an overt statement of his fear, an assertion that men let women dominate them.

Jimmy warms to his words so much that he comes to realize that what is lacking in his life is something to die for. It is the absence of a 'good cause', something to rouse him and others from their apathy. He says that an atomic war would only mean death for nothing worthwhile, since he sees nothing worthwhile in the present world. He is disenchanted with the quality of life, particularly with what he sees as the limitations of his own existence, hence his cynical remarks in the wake of Cliff's threatened departure. This cynicism is further seen in his remarks that Cliff might just as well surrender and be taken over by a woman since life is so pointless. Because of what he is – aggressive and unpredictable in temperament – Jimmy is hurt further when Helena tells him that Cliff has already confided in her his intention of leaving. We feel sympathetic to Jimmy: after all, Cliff is his friend. He is so moved that he undertakes some sympathetic analysis of Cliff, referring particularly to his capacity to feel and his generosity of spirit. Prior to that he had suggested that they go out for a drink, and in jocular fashion had told Helena to get 'glammed' up, an instance of his volatile capacity for a change of mood. When they are alone we see Jimmy's appraisal of their relationship of passion and conflict. He defines Helena's actions and motives probably much better than she could herself, but his tiredness and his cry for help, his begging her not to let anything happen to change what they feel, again shows his vulnerability and the deep pathos of his situation. This is seen too in his expressed wish to escape from his way of life with her: he is here influenced by memories and the fact that Cliff is going. To Jimmy, a new start seems practicable: meanwhile he indulges his sexual passion for Helena, contemplating an evening spent drinking followed by inspired love-making.

But whenever Jimmy is exultant or on the edge of happiness it seems that life's little ironies put him down: here the dramatic return of Alison creates what is described in the stage directions as a *stunned pause*. Jimmy's response is apparently a cruel one. He indicates to Helena that a friend of hers has come to see her. It is as if he is cutting out his past life with Alison (he who has been so intense about the past in his own life), but we must allow for the suddenness and unexpectedness of Alison's entrance. Jimmy is sensitive. The fact is that he is lost for words here perhaps because he still sees Alison as having betrayed him (and perhaps too he feels guilty over Helena).

The final scene of the play finds Jimmy again off stage but, as previously, very much part of the action, since his trumpet-playing is always present. This is the background to the conversation between Alison and Helena. We wonder at his own determination and obstinacy in keeping it up. It appears to be an assertion of defiance and independence, for assuredly he knows that the two women are talking about him. It is a running reminder anyway, and it finally drives Helena to desperation. Jimmy's influence and fascination are obvious anyway, with Alison nostalgically recalling the pipe and Helena making a cup of tea that is a good one, something she learned from Jimmy.

Part of the attraction that Jimmy possesses is undoubtedly the fact that he is different. The conversation between Alison and Helena is largely about Jimmy's character, and it ties in admirably with what we have already learned. When Jimmy says that there are no good causes left to fight for, we find Helena asserting and Alison agreeing that he was born out of his time. This exactly defines his own situation, and in his own terms too. But Helena extends this, and we can't help feeling that she is right when she says that Jimmy does not know who he is or 'where he is going'. This is truthful, because Jimmy appears to be rootless: what roots he has are in the past, nurtured by loyalty, anguish, anger. His present with the sweet-stall (which he was going to give up to go off with Helena anyway) seems to be another act of defiance. Where does he belong? That is the identity-crisis question which Helena describes. When she goes on to say that Jimmy will never achieve anything she is applying to him the set middle-class values which he despises. 'Getting on' in the world, being what is now called 'upwardly mobile', is a major concern of conventional society. To have status, salary, position, a good house, material possessions, all these are the measures of that society. Jimmy is completely outside this range, since he does not conform and, as far as we can see, has no intention of doing so anyway. Osborne has cast Jimmy as a rebel without a cause, but there is no reason to suppose that he would 'betray' his inheritance. Helena is conventional underneath: her measures cannot apply to Jimmy, who has his own.

When Alison observes that Jimmy needs both a mother and a tart (my brief paraphrase) she is in fact underlining both his vulnerability and his contempt for convention, though she does suggest that he is given more time. It seems that she feels he may eventually be forced to conform, as most of us do in life, or at least that he may reach some kind of maturity about his own needs. When Helena summons Jimmy we note that, although he still speaks of Alison as 'her friend', he is obviously moved by the sight of her and her apparent suffering. He knows at once that Alison has lost the child, shrugs off the loss to himself because he has had other losses, but responds sensitively to Alison's statement that this is her first. He does not say anything at once, but we know that he feels she has entered into personal suffering. This registers immediately. And he must recall, as we do, that this is what he wished for her: now he has to face the terrible and self-wounding recognition that his wishes have come true. When Helena tells Jimmy that she is leaving although she loves him – she even says that she will never love anyone else – Jimmy is quiet and merely acknowledges what she says. It is a surprising reaction, if only because we are not used to seeing Jimmy lost for words. However, we understand the reaction once he begins to speak, for his nod signifies his recognition that Helena is opting out, turning away from the suffering which is the accompaniment of living, turning from her guilt feelings, turning back to the conventional life where she will be able to control what happens. Jimmy knows that love involves both suffering and courage. His theme is that if you are not prepared to accept this, you will never be a complete human being, you will never really be alive. That quality of life is so essential to him that he turns on the silently suffering Alison and tells her off for not sending flowers to Hugh's mum's funeral. The accusation is that she has betrayed him; we see that he is revealing to her his own need for her, his essential loneliness. It is a cry, and he even acknowledges that he misinterpreted her when they first met, feeling that the quality of relaxation she displayed was the result of life experience.

What he appears to have seen was Alison's somewhat self-contained apathy. But Jimmy is now looking at an Alison who *has* experienced suffering, and his appeal to her, his vulnerability and his need, moves her in a terrible way: she reveals that she has at last become what he wanted. Jimmy is moved beyond reason, unable to cope with what he has demanded and provoked: the result is that he leads them both into the fantasy world of escape where life can no longer injure them and where they will be (temporarily) safe and all in all to each other. Osborne gives the final ironic twist to Jimmy's character. He, who has demanded from others the need to suffer the pain of life, now finds the experience of it in Alison rather too much for him.

ALISON

We are told that there is a quality of elusiveness about Alison, and her 'well-bred malaise' reflects the apathy which Jimmy tries so hard to puncture, to force her into definite response and commitment. The natural breeding, the fact that she looks elegant in Jimmy's shirt, is a deliberate emphasis of the difference, and certainly the class difference, between them. She is beautiful, but the most arresting aspect of her according to Osborne's stage directions is her eyes. The implication is that by looking at them one *should* feel that she is incapable of deception: as the play demonstrates, she isn't, and this is very important to our understanding of her. She can't bring herself to tell Jimmy about the baby, she lets Helena persuade her to return home to have it, and then leaves before Jimmy returns.

Her initial responses show how weighed down she is by life, for her remarks are off-hand, seem to lack concentration. She admits that she hasn't been listening. Her saying early on that she can't think is another admission of the pressures of domesticity. Perhaps we should bear in mind, knowing what we learn later, that even here she is brooding about her pregnancy and the difficulty of telling Jimmy.

She does respond, however, to the affectionate kidding of Cliff, and it is soon apparent that he provides her with sympathetic solace. She seems too to want to be alone, perhaps to give herself time to think: this is seen where she suggests that Jimmy and Cliff go to the pictures together. Alison shows some spirit (and perhaps a little bitterness) in invoking the memory of Madeline. There is an edge of jealousy in what she says. Several times we get the feeling that she is near breaking-point, and once she begs Jimmy not to carry on. This only moves him to a Nigel-battering sequence which causes her to say that she'll go out of her mind. She doesn't, and turns to the practicality of ironing Cliff's trousers, maintaining her jocular tone as she hands them back.

There follows a moment in which she is able to show her warm feelings for Cliff. It is a short interlude. Then comes the horseplay in which her arm is burned. She shouts at Jimmy, and it is obvious that in addition to the physical pain she is suffering mental anguish, telling Cliff that she can't take much more. She confides in Cliff, telling him how she deliberately annoys Jimmy by pretending not to listen to what he says (p. 28). She trusts Cliff, and tells him that she is pregnant. She has obviously thought much about her situation, and we are moved when she tells Cliff that she fears that Jimmy will suspect her motives in becoming pregnant: she feels that he will feel trapped. She refers to the past: she was conventionally moral before marriage, another area of conflict between herself and Jimmy.

Alison has a little devilry in her. When Jimmy comes back in she makes sure that she has her arms around Cliff. Even here she may be playing up to Jimmy somewhat despite his sarcasm when he sees them: for this is a visual demonstration of one of his needs, which is to feel that his friend and his wife get on well. When Cliff goes out they escape into their fantasy of the squirrels and bears, a great relief for Alison at this moment of tension as she nurses her secret. It is part of getting Jimmy into the right frame of mind through this mutual indulgence, but fate in the form of Cliff returns and prevents her from telling Jimmy about the baby. The moment passes, and with her announcement that Helena is coming to stay, Jimmy's cruel wish that she should have a baby which will die stuns her. It is made the more poignant for her because the words are said in ignorance of her real state. At the end of the act she is so deeply shocked that she cannot speak. Perhaps at the back of our minds we wonder if she could have put Helena off, but decided not to because she needs the security of another woman's presence herself.

The comfort she gets from Helena being there is obvious at the beginning of the second act. She is disconcerted when Helena asks if Cliff is in love with her. Her reply shows how much she appreciates the warmth of her relationship with Cliff, the sympathetic security she has without the frenzy of sexual demands. Alison also feels moved to open up about her life to Helena, and in doing so she shows how fully she understands Jimmy and his strong loyalties in the past and the present. She herself fills in the details of that past for Helena's benefit (and the audience's too), describing her sense of loss at being cut off from all she has known, but admitting that it was her own fault. She is keenly aware of her own class background, feeling that she was a hostage to Jimmy and Hugh. She tells of the humiliations she has suffered at their hands. She describes her strong feelings of sexual attraction to Jimmy. She admits that she is snobbish over Hugh's mother, but there is a refreshing self-honesty about her account. Her identification with the bears and the squirrels strikes a genuine note of pathos. Having decided to go to church with Helena, who has already got at her to leave Jimmy, she endures Jimmy's next verbal assault (particularly the more-than-over-the-top one on Mummy), nearly breaks, but has just sufficient in reserve to tell Jimmy the searing home truth about himself – that he has to have his suffering. Eventually she does go to church with Helena, but we see how divided she is: it anticipates her serious leaving of Jimmy but here, significantly, she wavers.

We next see her in conversation with her father, who tells her a few home truths about herself too. She learns that she may be in part to blame for what is wrong in the relationship between Jimmy and herself. She resents the implication that she is inclined to 'sit on the fence', since she feels that she showed a bold decisiveness in marrying Jimmy, that she was strong-minded enough to know what she wanted. She feels that Jimmy threw down a challenge which she accepted. Alison looks back in anger herself, pointing out that she has been 'on trial' with Jimmy. She shows her acuteness too when she tells her father that he is upset because everything has changed, whereas Jimmy is upset because it hasn't. When she picks up the squirrel we feel that she is temporarily turning towards her life with Jimmy. Yet she seems surprised that Helena is staying (is Alison naïve on some counts?), is obviously moved at saying goodbye to Cliff: we feel that she is so moved that the letter – the conventional thing – is all that she can manage, and that confrontation would undermine her decision. There is another point, and that is that by making the break in this way she is perpetuating their conflict. She must know that Jimmy will be very angry.

Alison disappears from the action once she leaves with her father, only to reappear at the end of the first scene of the third act. She seems ill and run-down. In the second scene we see at once just how strong her attachment to Jimmy is, for the associations with his pipe and the memories this brings show how strong the ties are. She is as divided as ever, for she feels guilty (at coming back) yet she is looking back, not in anger, but in a kind of wistful and nostalgic way to her life with Jimmy in the very room where she is now talking to Helena. She displays a determined and admirable common sense in her attitude towards marriage. We sense her hope, almost relief, perhaps both, when Helena says that she is going to leave Jimmy. Alison knows that Jimmy needs both mother and lover in a woman. When Helena faces Jimmy with what has happened – the death of the child – it is Alison's emotions which move us when she says that this was her first real loss.

With the departure of Helena Alison has her outstanding moment in the play. Her impassioned speech shows that she needs Jimmy as much as he needs her. She is doing just what he wants her to do – grovel – because she has passed through the suffering which he had demanded of her, threatened her with, wished for her. We feel here that she is responding to Jimmy's vulnerability and his need. Her last action is infinitely pathetic: she is lover and mother to Jimmy, in conflict and in fantasy.

HELENA

Helena does not appear until the beginning of Act II. Stage directions here are certainly pointers to her personality, the 'royalty of middle-class womanhood' having Osborne's individually ironic tone. We have been prepared for Helena in a way by Jimmy's rage at Alison's announcement that she will be staying. In presence she is not merely impressive (Osborne's word) but an actress who lives life by putting on a performance. We might compare her with Jimmy on this account. She is in unfamiliar surroundings here and we sense that the arguments, the daily conflicts, are beginning to eat into her. Helena's first words reflect her conscious assumption of authority in preparing the meals, and her conscious adjustment of her standards to the 'primitive' conditions.

She soon reveals that she is both fascinated and repelled by Jimmy. Her remark about the trumpet betrays her fear of him, but that fear is allied to the inner excitement that she feels. It seems likely that she has not experienced such aggression before. Helena is inquisitive, and likes to know, and thinks that she knows, what is going on, hence her questions about Cliff and Alison being in love. Alison's reply hardly satisfies her, since by her standards the kind of relationship between Alison and Cliff – warm, friendly, sympathetic – should carry a sexual overtone, should be of the nature of an affair. Her reply to Alison shows her own sexuality, and prepares us for her later-revealed passion for Jimmy.

At first Helena's role, despite her personality, is a somewhat passive one; her function, like ours, is to listen to Alison telling the story of how she came to meet Jimmy and the nature of her experiences with him. Helena is horrified, as one would expect her to be, at the revelations of class aggression: she is amazed that Alison married Jimmy. Yet the fascination persists, for she is avidly taking in everything that Alison says about him. She outwardly rejects or disapproves of what she hears, but we sense that her need to hear it reveals a deeper feeling than she would care to admit.

When she has heard the story and knows that Alison is going to have a baby, Helena becomes more positive. She begins to take over, telling Alison that she (Alison) cannot go on living in this way any longer. Her first idea is that Alison must tell Jimmy that she is pregnant: she feels that this will bring Jimmy to a proper sense of his responsibilities. She is bewildered, registering blankly when Alison tells her about the bears and the squirrels: she uses a kind of middle-class vogue word – 'fey' – to indicate her doubts about Jimmy's sanity. She feels that Alison might fight Jimmy or get out: her role in the action has now changed and developed, and she is intent on bringing things to a head. This comes almost before she foresees it: the women's decision to go to church, a 'betrayal' as far as Jimmy is concerned, provokes a scene.

Before that Helena is well in command of herself, and is able to spar with Jimmy. Her middle-class clichés, as when she refers to Jimmy as 'a very tiresome young man', delight him. She shows strength of purpose and steadiness as the storm breaks about her head. Soon though she feels 'sick', experiencing contempt and hate at the ferocity of Jimmy's attack on Alison and her mother. When she threatens to slap Jimmy's face she is acting as she believes she should, but her confrontation with Jimmy undermines her own conventions and shows her the state of her own feelings.

While Jimmy is out taking the phone call Helena reveals her passion: she feels she could tear Jimmy's hair out, and she is also angered by the fact that Alison will be suffering in a few months' time, and all because of Jimmy. There is a terrible unconscious irony about Helena's words and feelings here in view of the fact that Alison's baby is to die. Typically, Helena attacks Cliff for not standing up to Jimmy, another conventional reflex on her part. She uses words like 'decent' and 'civilized' because they represent for her a standard way of life, like control of feelings, the exercise of good manners, for example.

But Helena suddenly reveals that she is devious and bossy at the same time. By sending Alison's father a telegram asking him to come and fetch his daughter, she has effectively taken over Alison's life. Without admitting it, she is pushing what she wants, though how aware of this she is at this stage we don't know: her relief when Alison agrees, though, is suspicious. And our suspicions increase when she announces that she is staying the night, nominally because she has an appointment in Birmingham the next day. It sounds thin. We feel that either she is guilty of contrivance – getting Alison out of the way so that she can have Jimmy – or that she doesn't know what she wants and is trying desperately to find out by staying. Cliff certainly believes that she wants Jimmy. Even as Alison is on the point of leaving, Helena continues to dominate, saying that she will tell Jimmy that Alison has gone, that is, if she is still there.

After Alison and her father have left, Helena appears to be on edge, even lighting a cigarette. And with Cliff's angry departure, she is left to herself. Significantly she picks up the bear, perhaps a subconscious indication that she wishes to possess Jimmy: after his angry response to Alison's letter, Helena calmly tells him that Alison is going to have a baby. This initiates the outburst which ends up with her slapping his face 'savagely'. It is the expression of her passion for him, and she follows it with the passionate kiss which shows her love.

Her role in the first scene of Act III shows how completely she has entered into, taken over, Alison's position. She seems poised as she irons and, at first, well able to cope with the situation: the stage directions show that she is relaxed. She stands up well to Jimmy's baiting about her religion, though she does try to get some relief from the continual diet of religion and politics which he enjoys. She has slotted into the routine of life so well that, although a little uncertain, she comes in on cue during the Flanagan and Allen parody. Her role now has duplications of Alison's earlier, even to the caring for Cliff's clothes, here his shirt. She appears to be passionately committed to Jimmy, her sexual need for him evident: but the return of Alison brings out the other side of her nature. This is her conventionalism, which demands that she release herself from a situation which she regards as morally indefensible. She upholds marriage, speaks of right and wrong and her own feelings of shame. Her insistence that she knows she has done wrong is followed by her explaining Jimmy, accounting for what he is and why: she falls back on the conventional judgements which she regards as the important measure of life: Jimmy will never achieve anything in the kind of society in which she will be living. Osborne underlines the importance of Helena's religion to her by having her confess to Alison: it is far from being outward observance merely, for she regards the loss of Alison's baby as 'a judgement on us'. She is still concerned and tender to Alison. She offers her more tea, shows that she is aware of her physical and emotional morale. She is determined and courageous, tackling Jimmy head on with her decision to leave.

When she leaves it is obvious that she is suffering greatly herself, but she cannot go on causing suffering to others. There is a curious mixture in Helena of selfishness and self-denial, crystallized in her last speech in the play (p. 93). That she loves Jimmy passionately is clear, and that she renounces him because she believes it is wrong is also clear: but we can't help feeling that the pain of living and loving, as Jimmy puts it, is too much for her.

CLIFF

Cliff, like Colonel Redfern, is not merely a stereotype, though he too has a functional role in the play. He is seen in contrast to Jimmy all the way through: he represents a largely uneducated standard of decency. We notice that he is conventional himself, even to the point of calling Colonel Redfern 'Sir'. Cliff is a warmly sympathetic character, particularly in his relationship with Alison. He gives her comfort and understanding, resents Helena taking over, but generally is too lethargic (Osborne's word in a stage direction) to do anything about it. In the first scene he tries to defend Alison from Jimmy's verbal assaults, though there is little he can do about them. He exchanges insults with Jimmy, on the whole in a jocular way, and perhaps enjoys his little tussles with him. Cliff is the friend who is essential to Jimmy: he comes to be necessary to Alison. He is aware that he is uneducated beside Jimmy, and in any case he cannot compete with him in terms of fluency or imagination. Yet even here he is not negligible, as we see from his fantasy about Jimmy 'interfering' with the cabbage and the tins of beans (p. 12).

Cliff's reference to 'Marchbanks' shows that he has acquired some education. He dislikes the rising tension between Alison and Jimmy caused by the mention of Madeline, and tries to head off the crisis by directing Jimmy's attention to the concert. All the time we are aware (although she is pressing his trousers) of his concern for Alison and the fact that she is tired. He is naturally affectionate to her despite Jimmy's presence. Cliff falls against Alison and she is injured. Afterwards he is all concern, massages her neck and kisses her on top of the head, without passion but with friendly and sympathetic warmth. He confesses to Alison that he doesn't feel that he could live by himself again, and there is too a hint of his feelings for her (and perhaps Jimmy) when he admits to getting 'fond of people'. At the same time he can't bear to watch what Alison and Jimmy are doing to one another. He seems bewildered by Alison's news that she is pregnant, and seems to need time to get used to it. Seeking a way out, he half asks if she could have an abortion: then he urges her to tell Jimmy, believing that the latter's love for her would condition his response.

Cliff takes some delight in self-mockery, in his working-class origins and his commonness. He also has the sensitivity to get Jimmy out of his mood when he comes back into the room after this accident, tugging Jimmy so that he falls, and then going out to get cigarettes so that Jimmy and Alison will be left together and she will be able to tell him about the baby. Unfortunately his return – bringing news of a phone call for Alison – comes too soon. He is still trying to placate Jimmy: he suggests going for a drink but, as Jimmy goes through Alison's handbag, he accuses Jimmy of always looking for trouble.

Later, Cliff tries to restrain Jimmy when he is launching a particularly vicious attack on Mummy (p. 53). He is so moved by what happens that he can't look at Alison or Jimmy. He even tells Jimmy to 'Dry up' when he picks on Helena. But as things get worse, and Helena turns on him for not intervening between Jimmy and Alison, Cliff has his finest moment in the play. He defends his position, fittingly in the imagery of war, saying that he has acted as a 'no man's land' between Jimmy and Alison, that he and his kind are used to fights like this, and that he loves the pair of them. It is a moment of quietness, sanity, acceptance: Cliff has not merely opted out, he has shown understanding and tolerance.

When Alison decides to go home with her father we once again have Cliff's obvious concern for her. He feels that she should wait for Jimmy's return and tell him herself. When he is left with Helena his tolerance is severely tested, and he becomes angry at her questioning of him. Cliff obviously suspects her motives, and it is his decision to give Helena the letter to pass on to Jimmy. His anger is seen here and in his outburst about picking up a girl that evening.

Cliff settles into the old routine with Jimmy, squabbling, indulging in horseplay, doing their own parody music-hall turn. Cliff is reluctant to give his shirt to Helena, agrees when Jimmy asks him to, but then tells Jimmy that things are not the same and that he intends to move on. After some *badinage* between them, he moves out of the play. Kindly, tolerant, feeling for Alison and Jimmy, Cliff's identity seems – obviously for dramatic purposes – to be wrapped up in theirs.

COLONEL REDFERN

Alison's father appears in only one scene. We have been led through Jimmy's statements – and Osborne's dramatic craftsmanship – to expect a stereotype: we get a briefly drawn but convincing individual. The stage directions indicate that he is uneasy in the situation of having to take Alison home. He too looks back to a world that has passed. He is living in a world which has no use for his authority. Part of his bewilderment is traced back to his daughter's marriage with Jimmy. This is because he feels – rightly – that Jimmy speaks a different language. He also ponders the strangeness of Jimmy's having a sweet-stall after his education. He believes that Jimmy is 'quite clever', but he qualifies it by hinting that Jimmy's way would not be the same as other people's. He shows that he has been interested to find out what Alison's living conditions were like, and then proceeds to a tolerant view of Jimmy's attitudes in the past, a fair consideration that he and Alison's mother were responsible for things going wrong. His revelation that his wife went over the top and employed private detectives to spy on Jimmy at least shows a conscience, and it shows also that much of Jimmy's bitterness – anger – is justified. He feels now that it would have been more dignified to have kept out of Jimmy's and Alison's affairs.

He believes that he and Alison were to blame for being indecisive (something that Alison cannot accept) and even suggests that she should not have written the letters that she did to them (another indication that what Jimmy has been saying is true). He even believes that Jimmy may be right in referring to him as a leftover from the Edwardian period. In a moving speech he reveals the loss of his past, the fact that everything has changed, that the place he had in the society he knew has gone. He, like Jimmy, though much more tired, is angry. Like Jimmy, he is displaced. He still wants to be sure that Alison knows what she is doing. We get the impression that he is under his wife's thumb, but that he tries very hard to grasp reality without an oppressive bias.

Commentary

BACKGROUND

In the post-war period the English theatre was in something of a
stagnant state. Many of the plays produced were middle-class
comedies for middle-class audiences, or farces calculated for their
popular appeal, or serious, conventional plays which never went
beyond the bounds of decorum in terms of language and situation.
There was an attempt to revive verse drama, notably by Christopher
Fry and T. S. Eliot, though the poetic element tended to reduce the
dramatic impact. The revival of classical plays also provided part of
the staple theatrical diet of the time. In America there was a much
more positive movement: Arthur Miller and Tennessee Williams
were ahead, in terms of social and political realism, of any playwrights
in this country before *Look Back in Anger*, and they were already
commanding a wider audience as their plays were translated to the
cinema and television screens.

But a movement away from stereotyped theatre had begun in
Germany through the influence of Bertolt Brecht (1898–1956).
Brecht's was a basically political drama, bent on exposing the forces at
work in society and, by so doing, bringing about political change.
Brecht's influence in this country led to the forming of the English
Stage Company (see p. 64), with its aim of developing new drama
independent of the commercial needs which had hitherto dictated it.
Young writers might attract young audiences instead of the almost
exclusively middle-aged and elderly theatregoers. One other name in
this pre-period stands out. *Waiting for Godot* (1953), Samuel Beckett's
original and innovative play, had been produced in England in 1955.
It is the first major break with convention: Margaret Drabble calls it a
'powerful and symbolic portrayal of the human condition as one of
ignorance, delusion, paralysis and intermittent flashes of human sympathy'. It is still, and will always be, vital theatre, capable of standing
many interpretations.

Running parallel to Osborne, preceding him slightly, is the emergence and influence of television. This was beginning to probe social, moral and political issues in documentaries and plays. In a sense, a play like *Look Back in Anger* brought the theatre into line with it. To compete with the expanding medium of television the theatre had to do what television was already doing by its sheer immediacy of impact. The time was ripe for the innovatory, direct, outspoken, socially conscious and explicit dramatists like Osborne, Arnold Wesker and Shelagh Delaney, to name three of the first wave. *Look Back in Anger* is immediate theatrical experience, the leading character clearly a product of his time who expresses himself about that time, giving voice to what many felt but could not articulate. In essence it is a dramatic social, moral and domestic record which has lived beyond its time because of its power to speak to, and perhaps for, all times. John Russell Taylor, in *Anger and After* (1962), explains how the English Stage Company came into existence. This is important because *Look Back in Anger* was the third play in its first repertory season at the Royal Court Theatre. Its director George Devine had the aim of encouraging new dramatists 'who would be delighted to write for the theatre if not put off by the prospect of having to battle with commercial managements to keep their play intact'. In fact the only outstanding new contribution he received at the time (after an advertisement inviting plays had been inserted in the *Stage*) was *Look Back in Anger*. This was variously reviewed, the outstanding acclamation from Kenneth Tynan in the *Observer* calling it 'the best young play of its decade'. Taylor observes that after an extract from *Look Back in Anger* was shown on television it attracted larger audiences: he also stresses that the time was just right, with the Suez crisis and the Hungarian one contributing to the mood of protest and to a 'grim political consciousness'. Its success effectively established the Royal Court 'as the London home of young drama'.

STRUCTURE AND THEMES

The three-act play is an established form, and in using it Osborne keeps to a straightforward chronology. Time passes between each act, though within the structure the title of the play is borne constantly in mind. The looking back is the running motif of the play. For example, Jimmy looks back to his dying father, Alison tells Helena the story of how she met and married Jimmy, and the Colonel indulges his nostalgia for the East. It has been rightly pointed out that *Look Back in Anger* is a well-made play, belonging to the 'solid, realistic tradition'. Where it departs from that tradition and establishes its own is in the language of the characters and the characters themselves, as we have seen from the section *An Account of the Plot.* The structure of the play and the clear expression of its themes are interwoven, as will be seen below.

The first act establishes the situation in the domestic and the social sense: it also establishes the setting which constitutes the whole play. The dialogue is dramatic, often violent; there is an exploration of relationships, some humour, action (the horseplay in which Alison is hurt), the news of Helena's phone call. There is plenty of looking back, as we have seen, but there is also much looking across, at the various aspects of contemporary life, for instance. It looks forward, with devastating irony, in Jimmy's expressed wish that Alison should have a child which would die, something which is to be a fact later. Suspense is maintained throughout the act, through the language, Jimmy's uncertain mood, the weariness (and worry) of Alison, Jimmy's aggression, the horseplay already mentioned and the wit, the repartee, the biting provocation. The feeling of uncertainty is intense, seeming to reflect the state of the world outside: Jimmy and Alison epitomize the class differences in a class-conscious society. The horseplay, the verbal assaults, are expressive of frustration and boredom, of disillusion with life, at least in Jimmy's case. Already we feel that the themes of *conflict*, *loyalty* and *friendship* are present: they are to be re-echoed throughout the play with clever variations. For example, Jimmy's diatribe against women, apart from showing his fear also shows him delighting in *conflict*, which he can't live without. There is Cliff's *friendship* for Alison and his *loyalty* in friendship to Jimmy. Always present is the theme of *anger*, which emanates largely from Jimmy but which is also present in the other characters on occasions. Apart from the past, Jimmy is directly angered by the evils (as he sees them) of contemporary society and the apathy of individuals. Linked to these is the theme of *escape*. In this act it is seen in the fantasy of the bears and the squirrels, and Jimmy's escape from the scene he has created when Alison is injured. Alison's escape from telling Jimmy she is pregnant hints that Cliff can no longer take the conflicts he witnesses daily and may have to get away.

Some critics have described the play as 'muddled'. To me it seems clear-cut, directly and firmly structured with a series of crisis points which never let the dramatic tension flag. Alison telling Cliff of her pregnancy involves the audience or reader in sympathetic concern – we have seen enough of Jimmy to share her doubts about his reaction. And our concern is *real*, spontaneous, not sentimental as in so many plays when a baby is mentioned. Osborne's craftsmanship, as I have emphasized, is apparent at every turn. Cliff urges Alison to tell Jimmy about the baby. After a comic sequence in which Cliff plays the fool as a means of easing the atmosphere, Cliff leaves so that Alison has her opportunity. This comic sequence is followed by Jimmy's concern for Alison, his expressed sexual desire for her and her response which leads them to the haven of their fantasy. Cliff's re-entry aborts the opportunity, his announcement of the phone call unwittingly brings back the critical tensions and provokes Jimmy into revealing his *insecurity* (another of the play's themes): this is exemplified here when he searches Alison's bag. There follows, on her return, his terrible wish which has already been examined.

By the end of the first act we have a clear insight into the domestic situation. The characters who are yet to appear, Helena and Colonel Redfern, are already in our consciousness through Jimmy's abrasive account of them. The ending of the act, with Alison about to say something, or to break, or both, and Jimmy's final, terrible words leave us on the edge of a frightening, uneasy tension. The dramatist has to give us immediacy and expectation as his play unfolds: by the end of this act Osborne has given us both in full measure.

Act II is just as clearly structured and the themes are reiterated, emerging in various forms. I have stressed through this commentary the importance of the stage directions (though Osborne himself has referred to some of them as 'irrelevant'), and certainly they are integral to the overall structure. They underline the main themes too. We observe the *friendship* between Alison and Helena: we might ponder on the motives of Helena later in wiring Alison's father to fetch her home. Is this friendship? Loyalty? *Loyalty* plays a large part in Alison's account of Jimmy (it is called 'allegiances') and she stresses her *friendship* with Cliff, which Helena would like to think was something more. Alison's demonstrations of Jimmy's *loyalty* are seen first in his attachment to Hugh (linked later to his response to Hugh's mother having a stroke). Note how his structuring enables Osborne to establish perspective: it is right in Jimmy's eyes for him to be loyal to Hugh's mother, but it is not right for Hugh to turn away from being a rebel or for Alison to let her friend Helena stay with them. That, as far as Jimmy is concerned, is *betrayal*, perhaps the most important word in his vocabulary.

Alison's retrospect on Jimmy again fits neatly into the structure. Having seen him in action throughout the first act, we want to know about his past, what made him as he is. And she provides us with an account which contains some explanation but not all: the imagery of war and conflict is there in the account, underlining the distance between Jimmy, Hugh and the upper-class party-going areas which they invade. Osborne also gives us Alison's response to Jimmy as she first sees him. This humanizes him, sexualizes him, stresses both his vulnerability and his attraction. Osborne is showing us how relationships develop and how they change, what they become in the claustrophobia of domestic life: this is perhaps the saddest part of the thematic content of *Look Back in Anger*.

Helena symbolizes the theme of *conflict* in her way too, telling Alison that she must fight Jimmy or leave. Helena's own conflict is within, the fascination and repulsion for Jimmy pulling her each way. And just as Jimmy dominates in his loud and non-stop talking way, so Helena dominates in hers, arranging for Alison to go home to have her baby and taking the necessary step to see that she does. Moreover, it is undoubtedly Helena's influence that makes Alison observe one of the conformities of the past, that of going to church, which, for Jimmy, constitutes betrayal. This provokes not merely the attack on Helena but an even more savage one on Alison's mother as the emblem of religious and social conformity and class superiority. The terrible *anger* informs the rest of the scene, and the look back to his father's dying, with Jimmy aware of his past impotence. The note of betrayal is sounded once again. His mother showed pity, but Jimmy was the one (in his own eyes of course) who cared. We get the feeling that Jimmy's fear of women may well have been conditioned by his mother's behaviour. The betrayal associations surface immediately after this with his calling Alison 'Judas': Cliff's loyalty to and friendship with Jimmy and Alison balance this when he tells Helena how much he cares for them both and how things have worsened since she (Helena) came. The end of the scene is again climactic. Alison will not go with Jimmy to Hugh's mother: he buries his face in the covers afterwards.

The sense of structure, of timing, from the exposition of the first part to the various climaxes of the second part of this scene is fine art, considered craftsmanship. It is not muddled but oppressively direct: consider the fact that Jimmy's loyalty will send him to Hugh's mother, who is dying, and that in his absence Alison will go home. Scene ii is immediately effective, providing comparison and contrast where we least expected it, namely in the person of Colonel Redfern, who is refreshingly unstereotyped. His attitudes towards Jimmy and towards his own past and the present are individual but fit into the themes we have observed – of conflict, of anger. If his anger is less passionate than Jimmy's it is just as real, for he has, in his own mind, no place in contemporary society. His contrasting perspective even apportions some of the blame for the past to himself and his wife, and for the present to Alison.

Helena's revelation that she is staying again raises the question of *loyalty* (and *friendship*), while Alison's writing the letter is a form of *betrayal*, as is Cliff's avoidance of Jimmy, though on a much more common and understandable level. The scene ends on the familiar but dramatically effective climactic note. Fascination has overcome repugnance, betrayal has overcome friendship, with expectation maintained at the highest possible pitch. And Jimmy too is involved in betrayal, though he would regard it as a conventional one, for he now knows about the baby. His anger erupts, embraces Helena, and afterwards becomes vulnerability and despair.

The structural coherence, the continuing themes, are bound together in the last act. In the 'well-made play' the last act is obviously geared to the resolution of situation and plot. Osborne keeps to that pattern admirably. We move forward in time several months, with a clever duplication of situation, as I have indicated earlier (see p. 31). Cliff and Jimmy epitomize their friendship: to use words they would appreciate, they are in the old routine. Cliff is aware of difference, and doubtless his *loyalty* to Alison makes things not the same. The central theme of *disillusion*, which arches over the play, is seen again in the comments on the nature of society and its malpractices. The *satirical* tone, and Jimmy's *anger*, are well in evidence. The *escape* – the Flanagan and Allen parody – is there, and through it and Jimmy's range the class war is there too. Cliff's decision to leave is muted *betrayal* (we wonder how Hugh explained his decision to go abroad), and Jimmy displays again his fear-of-women repertoire. And at the end of the scene Alison's reappearance is in the climactic mode that Osborne uses so well. Again Osborne's dramatic sleight of hand is present. The *resolution* appeared to have arrived with Jimmy and Helena starting a new life together. The suddenness of change allows only for a quick curtain before the final resolution.

Alison has brought herself back by *loyalty* and the sense of her own *betrayal* of Jimmy. Helena realizes that by her religious and moral codes she has *betrayed* Alison. She, like Alison, is still in *conflict* with herself and Jimmy, the protagonist of conflict, is all the while present through his trumpet. With Helena's decision to go we are aware of these themes again – the *escape* which Jimmy is to translate as being from 'the pain of being alive'. And, with sublime irony, he finds himself locked into the bears and squirrels *escape* with Alison at the end. It is finely and satisfyingly done, real and not sentimental, immediate and searing. They did not live happily or unhappily ever after: but maybe, after their experiences, they lived.

Discussion Topics and Examination Questions

DISCUSSION TOPICS

Your understanding and appreciation of the play will be much increased if you discuss aspects of it with other people. Here are some of the topics you can consider.

1. How far is Cliff an important help to our understanding of the characters of Jimmy and Alison? Refer to particular incidents in the play to support your arguments.
2. Do you find Jimmy a sympathetic or unsympathetic character, or both? Be prepared to support or defend what you say by quoting from the play.
3. What do you find most interesting in *Look Back in Anger* and why?
4. Read the stage directions describing each of the characters carefully. How important are they to our seeing and understanding each character?
5. Why do you think the play is called *Look Back in Anger*? Again, look at the play to support your views.
6. For which of the characters do you feel most pity and why?
7. There are many literary and contemporary references in *Look Back in Anger*. Choose one set of references, and say how far it contributes to your appreciation of the play.
8. What aspects of *Look Back in Anger* do you find humorous and why?
9. Consider what Alison and Helena have in common with each other. Which of these two do you prefer and why?
10. Which incident in the play do you find the most exciting? Say why, and compare it with another incident to bring out its dramatic quality.

11. What do you learn of the period about which John Osborne is writing?

12. In what ways is Colonel Redfern different from what you expected? *OR* Although Mummy never appears, she's a powerful influence on the action. How far would you agree or disagree with this?

THE GCSE EXAMINATION

If you are studying for the GCSE examination you may find that the set texts have been selected by your teacher from a very wide list of suggestions in the examination syllabus. The questions in the examination paper will therefore be applicable to many different books. Here are some possible questions which you could answer by making use of *Look Back in Anger*.

1. Write about any book you have read where the story and action are dominated by one character.

2. In your chosen book, show how the arrival of an outsider influences the other characters.

3. Give an account of the main aspects of the period in which your chosen book is set.

4. Examine the presentation of the theme of conflict in any book you have studied.

5. For which character in the book you are studying do you feel most sympathy and why?

6. Write about the author's use of something sudden or unexpected in your chosen book.

7. With reference to any two characters, show how the author you have chosen uses contrast in his presentation of them.

8. Examine the use of humour *or* the author's creation of atmosphere in any book you are studying.

9. Give an account of a character who endures much suffering in a book you have read.

10. Examine any relationship in the book you are reading and show how it develops. Do you find it realistic or not?

11. Write an account of any dramatic incident in a book you are reading.

12. In your chosen book, write about the main qualities of the author's style – his/her choice of language, dialogue, images, etc. – and say how it affects your appreciation of the book.

FOR THE BEST IN PAPERBACKS, LOOK FOR THE 🐧

In every corner of the world, on every subject under the sun, Penguin represents quality and variety – the very best in publishing today.

For complete information about books available from Penguin – including Puffins, Penguin Classics and Arkana – and how to order them, write to us at the appropriate address below. Please note that for copyright reasons the selection of books varies from country to country.

In the United Kingdom: Please write to *Dept E.P., Penguin Books Ltd, Harmondsworth, Middlesex, UB7 0DA.*

If you have any difficulty in obtaining a title, please send your order with the correct money, plus ten per cent for postage and packaging, to *PO Box No 11, West Drayton, Middlesex*

In the United States: Please write to *Dept BA, Penguin, 299 Murray Hill Parkway, East Rutherford, New Jersey 07073*

In Canada: Please write to *Penguin Books Canada Ltd, 2801 John Street, Markham, Ontario L3R 1B4*

In Australia: Please write to the *Marketing Department, Penguin Books Australia Ltd, P.O. Box 257, Ringwood, Victoria 3134*

In New Zealand: Please write to the *Marketing Department, Penguin Books (NZ) Ltd, Private Bag, Takapuna, Auckland 9*

In India: Please write to *Penguin Overseas Ltd, 706 Eros Apartments, 56 Nehru Place, New Delhi, 110019*

In the Netherlands: Please write to *Penguin Books Netherlands B.V., Postbus 195, NL–1380AD Weesp*

In West Germany: Please write to *Penguin Books Ltd, Friedrichstrasse 10–12, D–6000 Frankfurt/Main 1*

In Spain: Please write to *Longman Penguin España, Calle San Nicolas 15, E–28013 Madrid*

In Italy: Please write to *Penguin Italia s.r.l., Via Como 4, I-20096 Pioltello (Milano)*

In France: Please write to *Penguin Books Ltd, 39 Rue de Montmorency, F-75003 Paris*

In Japan: Please write to *Longman Penguin Japan Co Ltd, Yamaguchi Building, 2-12-9 Kanda Jimbocho, Chiyoda-Ku, Tokyo 101*